JERUSALEM
THE TEMPLE MOUNT

To our beloved children,
Daniel, Nathaniel, Benjamin, Anna, Joel and their spouses
Born in Jerusalem (mostly)
Passionate lovers of the Holy City
Enthusiastic travelling companions
Excellent photographers
Willing helpers
Patient sounding boards
And now opening the eyes of others to the delights of Jerusalem!

JERUSALEM
THE TEMPLE MOUNT

LEEN & KATHLEEN RITMEYER

cartaJerusalem

First published in 2015 by
CARTA Jerusalem

Editor: Barbara Laurel Ball

Text © Leen and Kathleen Ritmeyer
Plans and drawings © Leen Ritmeyer
Photographs © Leen and Nathaniel Ritmeyer

Other photo sources:
British Museum — p. 24
Philip Evans — pp. 28, 30, 89, 90, 124
Israel Ministry of Defense — p. 40
Clare Ritmeyer — p. 47
Alexander Schick — pp. 60, 91
Obe Hokansen — p. 84
Matson collection — p. 97
Dan Bahat — p. 100
Nick Barnes — pp. 120, 121
Marcio Teixeira — p.134

Carta books are available at special discounts for bulk purchases for sales promotions, premiums, fund-raising, or educational use. For details contact:
Carta Jerusalem, Ltd.
18 Ha'uman Street, POB 2500
Jerusalem 9102401, Israel
carta@carta.co.il   www.carta-jerusalem.com

ISBN: 978-965-220-855-2

Printed in Israel

TABLE OF CONTENTS

CHAPTER THREE
A Tour of the Temple Mount Platform
Going Up to the Mountain of the House of the Lord

Appendices

PREFACE

It is the authors' sincere hope that this profusely illustrated guide book to the Temple Mount will help you to fully savor the experience of visiting a site that is truly without parallel and be embraced by its aura of power and sanctity. It is the culmination of years of academic work distilled into a user-friendly manual whose aim is to make the dry facts and stones come alive. If it can help you make this complex site more accessible and find your own personal spots for reflection, it will have fulfilled our vision.

Each of the six distinct areas connected to the Temple Mount is preceded by a "Useful Information" section. Each route has its own detailed tour map. Of course, the tours can be done in whatever order you choose to do them in, including or omitting as you like.

The specialized maps at the end of the book provide additional information if you wish to focus on a particular aspect of the Temple Mount. One unique, never before published, map gives New Testament references that will allow you to follow in the footsteps of Jesus and his disciples around the Temple. The plan of the cisterns and underground structures will give you an idea of the magnitude of the vast world that lies beneath the Temple platform. The map of the Islamic structures will acquaint you with the gems of Muslim architecture all over the platform.

These maps are even more valuable for the armchair travellers who, for whatever reason, cannot visit the Temple Mount, but who are there in spirit! They too can share the insights provided by this concise guide and gain a deeper understanding of why this miniscule speck on the globe that has caused more controversy than any other is so fascinating to many. They will also be indispensable on those occasions when, although you may be in Jerusalem, the political climate dictates that the Mount is closed and you are restricted to circumnavigating its walls.

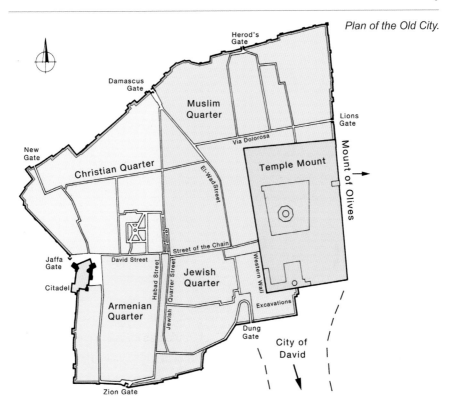

Plan of the Old City.

Incredibly, this is the first true guide of the Temple Mount to be published since 1925, when the Supreme Muslim Council published their 12-page *Brief Guide to al-Haram al-Sharif*.

You can use the plan above to help orientate yourselves with regard to directions.

Note:

This book tells the story of the Temple Mount that was built atop Mount Moriah. It does not extend to the city of Jerusalem in the various periods. Thus city walls or other structures in the vicinity of the Temple Mount have been omitted in the reconstruction drawings.

Leen & Kathleen Ritmeyer
August 2014

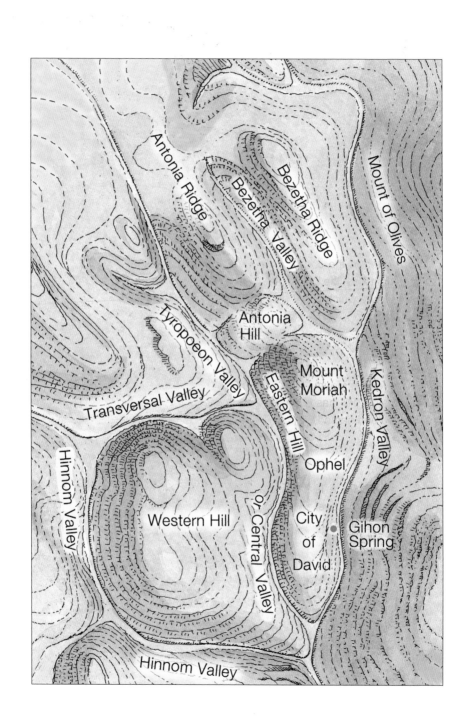

CHAPTER 1

A BRIEF HISTORY OF THE TEMPLE MOUNT

LOCATION

The Eastern Hill

An understanding of the location and topography of the Temple Mount is necessary in order to comprehend how the site developed over time. The mount itself is an unspectacular hill nestled in the Judean Mountains that separate the Coastal Plain from the Wilderness of Judea. Its location and that of the city which developed around it, at the heart of this range, inspired the psalmist to write: "As the mountains are round about Jerusalem, so the Lord is round about his people from henceforth even for ever" (Psalm 125.2). The northern part of this long narrow ridge known as the Eastern Hill is the Temple Mount.

The Eastern Hill has several spurs. The lowest of these was settled and named the City of David, after the king who conquered it. Between the City of David and the highest point of the Eastern Hill is a gentle incline known as the Ophel. To the north at the crest of the Eastern Hill is Mount Moriah, on which the Temple was built; it rises to 2,440 feet (743 m) above sea level and is visible today inside the Dome of the Rock. Moving northward, the ridge dips down, with a saddle separating it from a small peak of what was later called the Antonia Hill. To the north of the Antonia Hill, the Eastern Hill widens out into two ridges, separated by the Bezetha Valley. The western ridge is the continuation of the Antonia Hill, while the eastern one is generally known as the Bezetha Ridge.

The Central or Tyropoeon Valley, which originally separated the Eastern Hill from the Western Hill, is now so choked with rubbish as to be barely discernible. Ancient

(opposite) The topography of Jerusalem.

Jerusalem was protected by this valley to the west and south and by the Kedron Valley that separated it from the Mount of Olives to the east. The city was always vulnerable to the north, as there is no distinct valley on this side. The Western Hill (2,536 ft./773 m above sea level), on the other hand, was naturally fortified by the Transversal Valley on the north, by the Hinnom Valley on the west and south and by the Central or Tyropoeon Valley on the east. With this advantage, it was an obvious choice for settlement, but crucially lacked a water supply. It was the Gihon Spring, a perennial water source located in the Kedron Valley at the foot of the City of David that was the deciding factor in the choice of the Eastern Hill for the original city of Jerusalem. The city was later extended to include Mount Moriah on the north as the location of the Temple Mount. Like the rest of the surrounding hill country, the Temple Mount was composed of hard and soft limestone layers that generally dip down from north to south. The Mediterranean climate lent itself to the "terrace agriculture" practiced by those early settlers.

Charles Warren's topographical map of Mount Moriah.

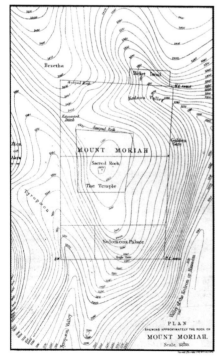

Mount Moriah

We can no longer see what Mount Moriah originally looked like. All that is visible today is its summit inside the Dome of the Rock. This is a small promontory, measuring 43×56 feet (13×17 m) and rising to a height of 9 feet (2.75 m) above its natural rocky surroundings. It must have appeared quite unique with its "pimple" or protuberance-like formation.

Although the mount is now concealed, we have inherited invaluable information from Charles Warren, the British engineer who explored Jerusalem in the 1860s on behalf of the Palestine Exploration Fund. He took bedrock levels wherever possible at entrances to cisterns and other places on the Temple Mount. With these data he produced a rock contour map, which has not been surpassed in

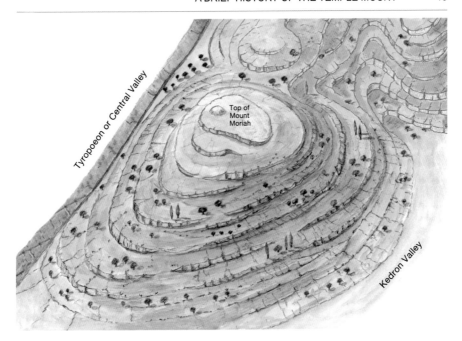

accuracy to this day. His measurements reveal that there was quite a flat area, 230×230 feet (70×70 m), surrounding the rocky protuberance. It was on this flat area that the Temple was built. From there, the mountain slopes down in all directions, with the steepest slope to the east towards the Kedron Valley and the side that sloped least towards the north, in the direction of the Antonia Hill. Although King Herod the Great extended the Temple in three directions, the preceding Temples were always built on Mount Moriah. And we will see later on that only the part of Herod's Temple Mount that was actually located on the mount was regarded as holy. Our illustration of the topography of Mount Moriah is based on Warren's rock contour map and uses the general configuration of the Jerusalem mountains, with the layered rock sloping from north to south.

Illustration showing the topography of Mount Moriah.

Mount Moriah in relation to the present-day Temple Mount.

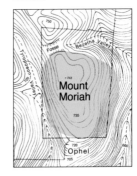

PRE-TEMPLE TIMES (4000–1000 BCE)

In the Beginning

It is with King David that Jerusalem and the Mount enter the flow of history as we know it. However, pottery remains

Who was Melchizedek?

Detail of painting "Meeting of Abraham and Melchizedek" by Dieric Bouts (1415–1475). Apart from Psalm 110.4, the mysterious figure of Melchizedek appears in the Hebrew Bible only once, in Genesis 14.18, where he is presented as both priest and king of Salem (identified as Jerusalem). This painting shows him blessing Abraham with bread and wine after the latter's rescue of his nephew Lot and defeat of the Mesopotamian kings. The Hebrew name Melchizedek can be translated as "King of Righteousness" (Hebrews 7.2).

of settlement from as early as the Chalcolithic period have been found in excavations on the southeastern spur below the Temple Mount. And many years prior to the familiar events recounted in Scripture, tantalizing snippets of the city's pre-Biblical history are revealed in clay documents from an earlier era. The Egyptian Execration Texts bore inscriptions cursing the names of cities and their rulers. One of these cities appears to have been Jerusalem. Dating from the twentieth to nineteenth centuries BCE, these texts testify to the Egyptian domination of the country during that period. Judging from the prominence of the name identified as Jerusalem (spelled *wsmm* and pronounced *rushalimum*), in these texts, it was an important Canaanite city-state at the time and, together with the other rebel cities mentioned, a thorn in the side of Pharaoh.

Most intriguing of all the early references to Jerusalem is a biblical passage in Genesis 14. This passage records the meeting of the patriarch Abraham and the King of Sodom with Melchizedek, King of Salem, "in the Valley of Shaveh which is in the King's Dale" (Gen 14:17). Salem could, of course, be connected etymologically to Jerusalem, but it is the undisputed location of the King's Dale (the site of the Pillar of Absalom, as described in 2 Sam 18.18), within the confines of the city of Jerusalem that clinches the identification. The King's Dale was an area of land in the Kedron Valley. It is conceivable that the sacrifice of a great number of animals that Abraham was asked to offer to God soon afterwards (Gen 15), also took place on nearby Mount Moriah. Strange as it may seem if we are used to seeing these historical episodes in isolation, the "binding of Isaac" on Mount Moriah, described in Genesis 22, must have taken place against the background of a bustling city on the southern slopes below.

Another brief glimpse into the fortunes of the city is given in letters found at the royal Egyptian archive of Tell el-Amarna. These date from the fourteenth century BCE and comprise correspondence between the Kings of Canaan, other neighboring kingdoms and their Egyptian overlords. The language in which they were written was Akkadian, the language of international diplomacy of the time. A number

of the letters to Pharaoh are from Abd-Khiba, the troubled King of Jerusalem (*Urusalim*). They describe the unsettled conditions that prevailed during this period of the decline of Egypt's power and are replete with intrigue, complaints and recriminations. Some fragmentary evidence of an Egyptian presence in Jerusalem at that time has come to light. However, because excavation on the Temple Mount is forbidden, the likelihood of finding traces of this period on Mount Moriah is slim.

The "King's Dale" in the Kedron Valley, looking northeast towards the Mount of Olives.

Jebusites

According to a biblical reference in Ezekiel 16.3, the origins of Jerusalem appear to be a mixture of Canaanite, Amorite and Hittite. However, the last pre-Israelite ruler of the city was Araunah the Jebusite. At that time, the mountain was used for growing wheat and barley, as attested to by the reference to the threshing floor of Araunah in 1 Chronicles 21.15. After God had brought a plague on Israel, the angel of the Lord, who was about to destroy Jerusalem, told King David to build an altar on the threshing floor. The angel was standing on higher ground, between heaven and earth as it were, most likely at the peak of Mount Moriah, while the threshing floor was on lower ground to the east, to exploit the prevailing westerly winds to separate the chaff from the

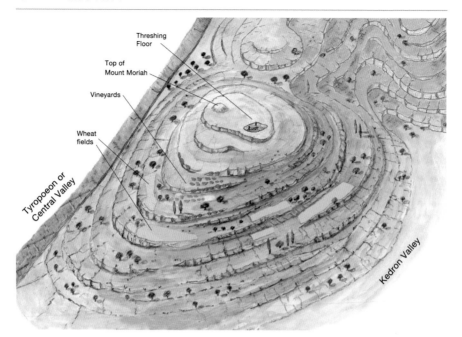

Threshing
Floor

Top of
Mount Moriah

Vineyards

Wheat
fields

Tyropoeon or
Central Valley

Kedron Valley

The Temple Mount at the time of the Jebusites.

grain. Threshing floors are never located on the very top of mountains, as the strong westerly wind would blow away both chaff and grain, but always on lower ground, usually on the eastern side. Jewish tradition maintains that David's altar was built (c. 980 BCE) on the same place that Abraham had erected his altar in preparation for the sacrifice of Isaac, before God intervened.

FIRST TEMPLE TIMES (1000–586 BCE)

The Temple of Solomon

At the beginning of his reign David brought the Ark of the Covenant from Kiriath-jearim to Jerusalem, the City of David. There it rested, presumably in a tent on the grounds of David's palace, until circa 967 BCE. The Ark was then moved into the new temple that was built on Mount Moriah by Solomon, the son of David. The Holy of Holies was placed on the summit of the mount, with the Temple facing east, toward the Mount of Olives. According to 1 Kings 6–7, the Temple consisted of two chambers, the Holy of Holies and the Holy Place. The Porch in front of the building was supported by two massive

*(opposite, above)
Development of
the Temple and
its building activity
through the ages.*

*(opposite, below)
The Temple Mount at
the time of Solomon.*

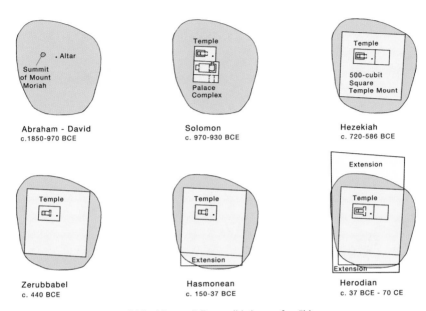

Abraham - David
c.1850-970 BCE

Solomon
c. 970-930 BCE

Hezekiah
c. 720-586 BCE

Zerubbabel
c. 440 BCE

Hasmonean
c. 150-37 BCE

Herodian
c. 37 BCE - 70 CE

bronze columns, named Yachin and Boaz (Hebrew for "He will establish…In strength"). Carved cherubim and palmettes

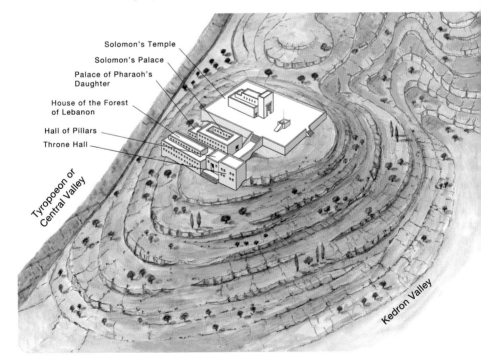

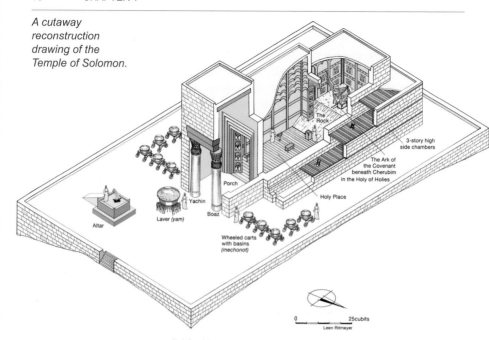

A cutaway reconstruction drawing of the Temple of Solomon.

3-story high side chambers

The Ark of the Covenant beneath Cherubim in the Holy of Holies

The Rock

Holy Place

Porch

Yachin

Boaz

Laver *(yam)*

Altar

Wheeled carts with basins *(mechonot)*

0   25cubits

Leen Ritmeyer

overlaid with gold graced the cedar-wood interior. Two doors, made of olive wood, separated the Holy Place from the Holy of Holies, where the Ark of the Covenant stood. Around the Temple, a three-story-high wooden structure was built for storage. In front of the Temple, on the place sanctified by the earlier altars, stood a brass altar, and to the east of the Temple façade was an enormous bronze laver, with five

What did the Queen of Sheba see?

Solomon built a resplendent palace complex adjacent to the Temple. It consisted of his armory, the House of the Forest of Lebanon, a Hall of Pillars, the Porch of the King's Throne, the King's House and the house of his wife, Pharaoh's daughter. On the visit of the Queen of Sheba to Jerusalem (1 Kings 10), the Ascent which Solomon built from this complex up to the Temple, was one of the things that inspired her awe.

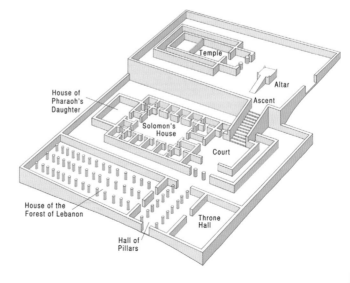

Temple

Altar

Ascent

House of Pharaoh's Daughter

Solomon's House

Court

House of the Forest of Lebanon

Throne Hall

Hall of Pillars

smaller moveable washbasins situated on either side of the Porch. This sacred compound was surrounded by a wall that formed the Temple court.

The Temple Under the Later Kings of Judah, to Hezekiah

Soon after Solomon's death, his kingdom was divided between Judah and Israel (925 BCE) and a few years later his magnificent Temple was ransacked by Shishak, King of Egypt. The Temple was again looted during the reign of Athaliah, daughter of a king of Israel and wife of King Jehoram of Judah. After the death of her son Ahaziah, she seized the throne in Jerusalem. Joash, the only royal heir to survive her murderous purge, sought donations from all the people of Judah to repair the damage. A massive earthquake that occurred in the last year of King Uzziah's reign again destroyed parts of the Temple. The three-storied construction and the Porch suffered heavy damage and King Ahaz caused further destruction by smashing all the bronze implements of the Temple, including the lavers and the two massive columns that supported the Porch.

The name of King Hezekiah appears on a seal impression with a depiction of a two-winged beetle. Inscription at bottom reads: lhzqyhw 'hz mlk, "(Belonging) to Hezekiah (son of) Ahaz, king (of)" while the inscription is completed above with the word yhdh, "Judah".

The Temple Mount at the time of the later kings of Judah.

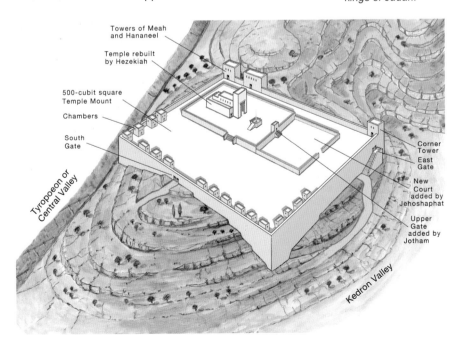

Towers of Meah and Hananeel

Temple rebuilt by Hezekiah

500-cubit square Temple Mount

Chambers

South Gate

Tyropoeon or Central Valley

Corner Tower

East Gate

New Court added by Jehoshaphat

Upper Gate added by Jotham

Kedron Valley

The Temple Mount today with indications of the 500-cubit-square Temple platform.

The Temple Mount in the Post-Exilic Period.

King Hezekiah (725–697 BCE) embarked on a major rebuilding program of the Temple, as reflected in the second and later accounts of the Temple construction in 2 Chronicles 3–4. In this passage, the two columns of the Porch are described as being 35 cubits high in contrast to a height of 18 cubits mentioned in 1 Kings 7. Instead of the three-story-high wooden construction that was built around Solomon's Temple, there is now an Upper Chamber above the original sanctuary. Other differences between the two descriptions show that Hezekiah not only rebuilt Solomon's Temple, but also redesigned it. Nevertheless, this Temple is still referred to as the First Temple that was destroyed by the Babylonians in 586 BCE.

Solomon's Temple had been set in a sacred court. A new court was added in the time of King Jehoshaphat (2 Chr 20.5), presumably east of the original Temple court. Judging by the architectural style of the archaeological remains in the Eastern Wall, King Hezekiah also surrounded this sacred complex with a massive 500-cubit-square artificial platform, called *har habbayit*. This measurement of 500 cubits has been preserved in the text of Mishnah *Middot* 2.1: "The

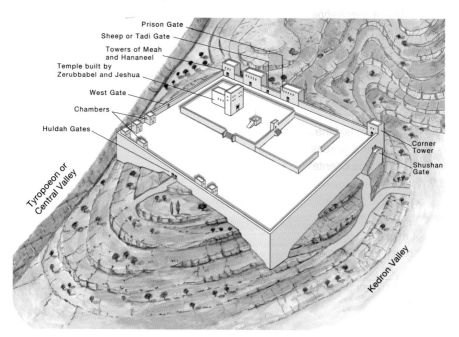

Prison Gate
Sheep or Tadi Gate
Towers of Meah and Hananeel
Temple built by Zerubbabel and Jeshua
West Gate
Chambers
Huldah Gates
Tyropoeon or Central Valley
Corner Tower
Shushan Gate
Kedron Valley

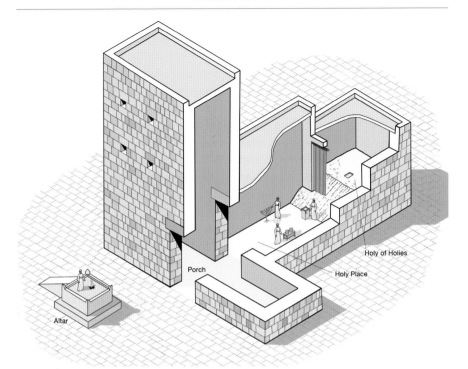

Holy of Holies

Porch

Holy Place

Altar

Temple Mount (*har habbayit*) measured five hundred cubits by five hundred cubits."

A cutaway reconstruction drawing of the Temple built by Zerubbabel and Jeshua.

SECOND TEMPLE TIMES (586 BCE–70 CE)

The Post-Exilic Period (536–332 BCE)

In the Post-Exilic period, the returnees from Babylon first built the altar and then laid the foundations of the Second Temple (536 BCE). There is no reason to doubt that these foundations followed the same orientation as the temple being replaced, as the foundation trenches were preserved in the Rock (as they are to this day). Due to the opposition of the local population, it took twenty years to complete the building. It did not match the splendor of its predecessor, as witnessed by the reaction of the older people who still remembered the First Temple (Ezra 3.12). The only information given about the Second Temple is that it was 60 cubits high and wide. These measurements presumably referred to its façade, as no measurements for length are provided.

The Hellenistic Period (332–152 BCE)

Josephus records in a somewhat fanciful manner (*Ant.* 11.325–339) a visit to the Temple by Alexander the Great after his capture of Gaza in 332 BCE. Here, the Jewish historian has him sacrificing in the Temple under the guidance of the High Priest. Although this may be mere legend, the story points to the perpetuation of the Temple services following their revival after the return from exile in Babylon. After the death of Alexander, Judea was governed by the Ptolemies of Egypt, who were tolerant of Jewish religious practice.

Around the end of the third century BCE, restoration work was carried out on the Temple Mount by the High Priest Simon, son of Onias. According to the apocryphal work of Ben Sira called *Ecclesiasticus* (50.1–3), the work is described as follows:

> It was the High Priest Simon son of Onias who repaired the Temple during his lifetime and in his day fortified the sanctuary. He laid the foundations of the double height, the high buttresses of the Temple precincts. In his day the water cistern was excavated, a reservoir as huge as the sea.

It is clear from the text that the bulk of these works consisted of the repair and strengthening of existing structures.

The Hasmonean Period (152–37 BCE)

Control of the city was won from the Ptolemies by the Greek Seleucids from Syria in around 200 BCE. The Seleucid dynasty was determined to force the Jews to accept Hellenism. It was the sacrifice of a pig on the Temple altar by the Seleucid ruler Antiochus IV Epiphanes that sparked off the revolt by the Maccabee brothers. Their bloodline evolved into the Hasmonean dynasty that established an independent Jewish state lasting from 164 to 63 BCE. The consecration of the Temple is still celebrated today by the Jewish feast of *Hanukkah*. Simon the Maccabee demolished the hated Akra, a fortress that the Seleucids had built to the south of the Temple Mount so that a Macedonian garrison could control the Jewish population. He then leveled the mountain on which it was built, incorporating the whole area into the

What is the difference between a *Menorah* and a *Hanukkiah*?

The Temple Menorah *(top) had seven branches, while the* Hanukkiah *used at* Hanukkah *has eight representing the eight nights that oil miraculously burned in the Temple.*
The lamp on the central ninth branch, which is called the shamash, *is used to light the others.*

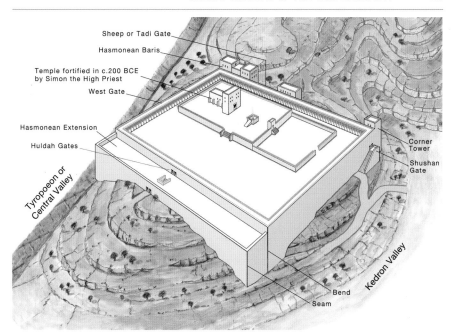

The Temple Mount in the Hasmonean period.

Temple Mount complex. After this extension to the south, the Temple was no longer square in shape.

Following the Maccabean rebellion, a fortress was constructed at the northwest corner of the square Temple Mount, to defend the mount against attacks from the north. It was called the *Baris*.

The Herodian Period (37 BCE–70 CE)

In 19 BCE the master-builder, King Herod the Great, began the most ambitious building project of his life, the rebuilding of the Temple in lavish style. To facilitate this, he undertook a further expansion of the Hasmonean Temple Mount by extending it on three sides, to the north, west and south. A visualization of this Temple Mount was made possible by combining the historical sources with the results of archaeological exploration. The main historical source is the first-century historian Josephus Flavius. His works, *The Jewish War* and *Jewish Antiquities*, although prone to exaggeration, are indispensable for this period. Also invaluable is the Mishnah, the earliest code of rabbinic law, written about 200 CE, particularly the Tractate *Middot*, which

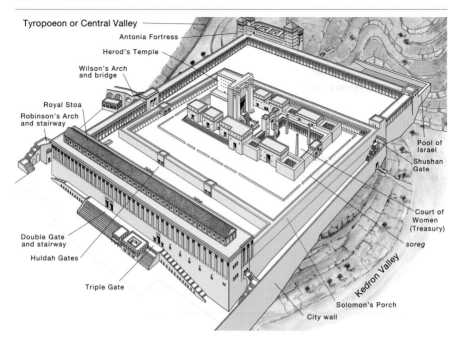

Tyropoeon or Central Valley
Antonia Fortress
Herod's Temple
Wilson's Arch and bridge
Royal Stoa
Robinson's Arch and stairway
Pool of Israel
Shushan Gate
Court of Women (Treasury)
Double Gate and stairway
soreg
Huldah Gates
Triple Gate
Kedron Valley
Solomon's Porch
City wall

Which cubit was used in the Temple?

deals with measurements. The New Testament adds further detail and context. All this was augmented by the results of the excavations to the south and west of the Temple Mount following the Six-Day War in 1967.

Herod extended the Eastern Wall of the Temple Mount to the north and south. The former extension required the filling in of a deep valley to the north of the pre-Herodian Temple Mount. The Shushan Gate remained the only gate in the Eastern Wall. Towers were erected at each corner and a large water reservoir was built at the northeast corner, the so-called Pool of Israel. At the northwest corner, the massive Antonia Fortress was built to protect the Temple against attacks coming from the north and to guard the mount in times of strife. The Western Wall, which had four gates, was placed some 82 feet (25 m) outside the square platform with its southwest corner built on the opposite side of the

An example of a cubit stick such as the one used by Eliezer ben Jacob to provide the measurements of the Temple for Rabbi Judah the Patriarch to complete the tractate of Middot (Measurements) in the Mishnah. In contrast to the commonly used short cubit of 18 inches/ 45 cm, this longer cubit of 20.67 inches/52.5 cm, known as the Royal or Sacred Cubit, was used in the construction of Israel's sanctuaries. (Photo: British Museum)

Tyropoeon Valley. The Southern Wall featured two gates, the Double Gate and the Triple Gate, often erroneously referred to as the Huldah Gates. Today's Temple Mount boundaries still reflect this enlargement.

Double colonnades, or porticoes, were built above the outer walls to provide shelter from the elements. On the south, a huge hall called the Royal Stoa, with four rows of columns, was erected. The pre-existing eastern portico that stood on the square mount was left unchanged. As it belonged to a pre-Herodian period, it was called Solomon's Porch.

(opposite page) The Herodian expansion of the Temple Mount.

The Temple of King Herod the Great

Herod's Edomite background made him suspect in the eyes of his Jewish subjects. Thus he had to find ways to allay

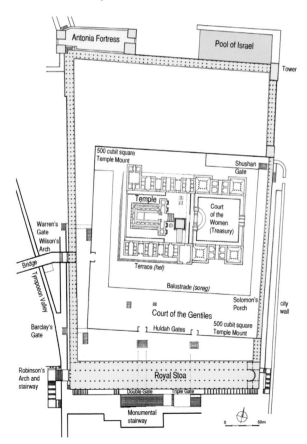

Plan of the Temple Mount in the Herodian period.

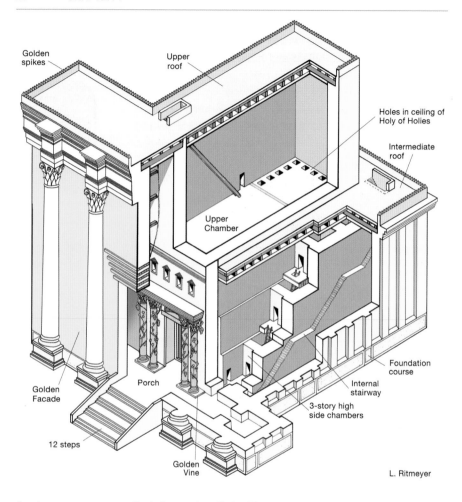

A cutaway reconstruction drawing of Herod's Temple.

their fears that if the Temple was dismantled, it might not be built again. This he did by assembling all the materials in advance. The stones for the Temple were quarried and prepared beforehand. A thousand wagons were made to transport them to the building site and ten thousand highly skilled workmen were selected for the construction. In addition, some priests were trained as masons or carpenters, whilst the daily ritual of the Temple proceeded side by side with the building.

Josephus called Herod's Temple "a structure more noteworthy than any under the sun" (*Ant.* 15.412) and in *War* 5.207–226 he gives this glowing description:

The sacred edifice itself, the holy Temple, in the central position, was approached by a flight of twelve steps. The façade was of equal height and breadth, each being a hundred cubits; but the building behind was narrower.… The exterior of the building wanted nothing that could astound either mind or eye. For, being covered on all sides with massive plates of gold, the sun was no sooner up than it radiated so fiery a flash that persons straining to look at it were compelled to avert their eyes, as from the solar rays. To approaching strangers it appeared from a distance like a snow-clad mountain; for all that was not overlaid with gold was of the purest white. From its summit protruded sharp golden spikes to prevent birds from settling upon them and polluting the roof.

The sources at our disposal combine to give the following picture of this magnificent structure. The foundation course of the Temple was a massive 6 cubits (10 ft./3 m) high. Twelve steps, in four sets of three with landings in between, led up to a Porch that was 100 cubits (172.2 ft./52.50 m) high and wide. Flanking the main entrance were four Corinthian columns with pedestals, bases and capitals. This feature of the façade is suggested by the four columns on representations of the Temple depicted on coins from the Bar Kokhba period. Details on these coins also suggest that there was an elaborate entablature decorated with rosettes and a wavy line resting on the capitals. Fragments of such rosettes were found in the Southern Wall Excavations. Josephus records that all around the top of the building were 1.7-foot- (0.5-m-) high golden spikes to prevent birds from fouling the façade. These spikes crowned a 5-foot- (1.5-m-) high wall. The façade was gold plated, but not the columns or the entablature. These latter elements were whitewashed once a year to keep them sparkling clean. From *Middot* we learn that inside the Porch, in front of the entrance to the sanctuary, stood a Golden Vine draped over four pillars.

The Temple proper, behind the Porch, was divided into the Holy Place and the Holy of Holies. Three stories of cells surrounded the Temple, making it 70 cubits (120 ft./36.75 m) wide. The upper story was 30 cubits (52 ft./15.75 m) wide.

Why did Herod's Temple continue to be called the Second Temple?

Solomon built the First Temple on Mount Moriah and after the Babylonian Exile, the Second Temple was built by Jeshua and Zerubbabel. That Temple has been renovated over time, especially by Simon the High Priest in 200 BCE. Although Herod built a new Temple, which rationally should be called the Third Temple, it was looked upon as an enlargement and embellishment of the existing Temple. Most importantly, the sacrifices were not interrupted during the building process.

These measurements make it possible to appreciate the description of the Temple in *Middot* 4.7 as "like to a lion... narrow behind and wide in front" and compares it with "Ariel", one of the biblical titles of Jerusalem, meaning "Lion of God."

The Holy Place measured 40 cubits (69 ft./21 m) high and 20 cubits (34.4 ft./10.50 m) wide. The seven-branched Lampstand (*Menorah*) stood in the south of this room, the Table of Shewbread (*ha-Shulchan*) in the north and close to the Veil (*ha-Paroketh*) that separated the Holy Place from the Holy of Holies, the Altar of Incense (*Mizbe'ach ha-Ketoreth*).

The Buildings of the Temple

The Temple stood inside the Temple Court (*azarah*) surrounded by buildings. On the south, twelve steps led up to the terrace (*hel*) that was constructed around these buildings. Three two-storied gate buildings stood on the north and south sides of the Temple, each having two small chambers in between them. At the northwest corner of the Temple Court stood the Chamber of the Hearth, where a fire was kept burning to keep the priests, who served barefoot, warm at night. This building had four rooms. The one in the northwest had steps leading down to an underground *mikveh*. The Chamber of Hewn Stone, where the Sanhedrin (the supreme Jewish legislative, religious and judicial body) used to meet, was located at the southeast corner of the Temple Court.

In front (i.e., east) of the Temple stood the Laver, the Altar and the Place of Slaughtering. On the east side of the Temple Court were two narrow courts, the Court of the Priests and the slightly lower Court of the Israelites. Only priests were allowed in the first court. Purified Israelite males had access to the second, where they could bring their offerings and observe the sacrifices. In the middle part of the Court of the Priests was a raised platform (the *duchan*) on which Levites used to sing the daily Psalm.

The massive Nicanor Gate on the east side of the Temple Court separated it from the Court

The Altar of Burnt Sacrifice (photo: Philip Evans).
The original portable Altar of Burnt Sacrifice built in the Wilderness of Sinai measured only 5 cubits (8.6 ft./2.63 m) by 5 cubits and was 3 cubits (5.2 ft./1.58 m) high. The dimensions of the altar in the Second Temple are thought to have been a massive 32 cubits (55 ft./16.8 m) by 32 cubits and 15 cubits (25.8 ft./7.87 m) high. On the model altar, three fires are shown, two of which were normally burning, one for the sacrifices, the other for the incense, with the third used for kindling.

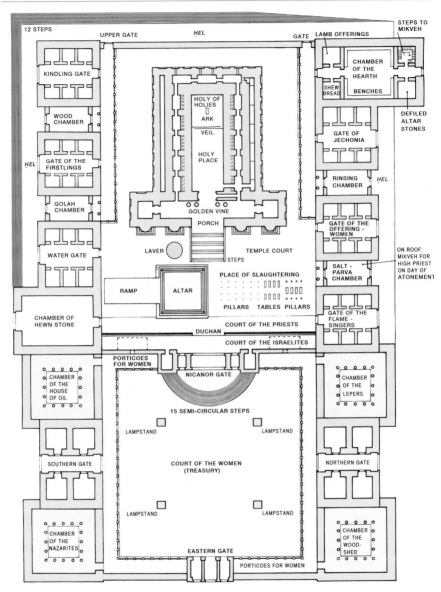

Plan of the Herodian Temple and its courts.

of the Women. The main gate had two large bronze doors that were made in Alexandria. The Mishnah attributes their arrival by sea to Jerusalem via Acre to a series of miracles. The gate had two smaller side gates: in the southern one, women who brought their sacrifice after childbirth were allowed to watch their being offered on the Altar.

Nicanor Gate (photo: Philip Evans).

The Court of the Women, known as the Treasury in the New Testament, was located on the east side of the Temple; it was the furthest that women could proceed into the Temple precincts. There were single gates that led into this court on each of the south, east and north sides. In front of the Nicanor Gate were fifteen semi-circular steps corresponding to the fifteen Songs of Ascents in Psalms 120–134. Here the Levitical Choir, accompanied by musicians, used to sing on special occasions. The tall golden lampstands that were lit during the Feast of Tabernacles (*Sukkot*) were a notable feature of this court. Surrounding the court were colonnades under which large boxes for monetary offerings were placed. Women were allowed on the balconies above these colonnades, where they could observe the rituals that took place in the Court of the Women.

Outside this Temple precinct, between the wall of the original 500-cubit-square platform and the *hel*, was a screen called the *soreg*, which bore inscriptions in Latin and Greek warning Gentiles and unpurified Jews from going any further.

The magnificent Temple compound formed the backdrop to much of Jesus' activity in Jerusalem, as recorded in the Gospels. The Book of Acts shows that the Temple became the central focus for preaching after his resurrection and it was later used in the Epistles as a metaphor to explain key concepts of Christianity.

In 70 CE, this splendid structure that had taken 46 years to build (John 2.20) was destroyed by the Romans. The only vestiges of the compound to survive the destruction were the four retaining walls that supported the Temple platform; the best known today is the Western Wall.

AFTER THE TEMPLE

The Temple Mount in the Roman Period (70–324 CE)

After the Roman destruction, the area of the Temple Mount lay desolate. In 130 CE, Emperor Hadrian began to build a Roman colony to be named Aelia Capitolina, on the ruins of Jerusalem. The name Aelia was given in honor of the emperor's family name, which was Aelius, while the name Capitolina honored the deities of the Capitoline triad: Jupiter, Juno and Minerva. Hadrian's actions precipitated the Revolt of Bar Kokhba ("Son of a Star"), which began in 132 CE. Some Jews regarded Bar Kokhba as the Messiah, in fulfillment of

The Temple Mount in the Roman period.

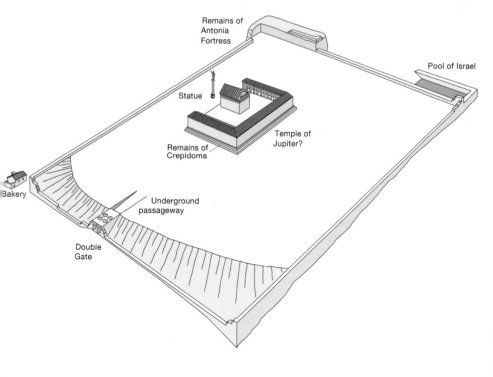

Remains of Antonia Fortress

Pool of Israel

Statue

Temple of Jupiter?

Remains of Crepidoma

Bakery

Underground passageway

Double Gate

Reconstruction of the Temple façade based on Bar Kokhba coins.

the prophecy of Numbers 24.17. Plans were made to rebuild the Temple and coins depicting it were struck (see previously, p.27). It is unclear how far these plans materialized. Following the suppression of the revolt in 135 CE, the pagan city of Aelia Capitolina became reality. Some historical sources indicate that during this period, a sanctuary to Jupiter was erected on the Temple Mount as were two dedicatory columns with statues of Hadrian and Antoninus Pius. The remains of three long steps that are no longer visible but were marked on Warren's plans, may have belonged to the southern part of the *crepidoma* (stepped platform) of this presumed temple. Jews were forbidden from entering the city on pain of death and Hadrian tried further to erase their connection to the Land by changing the name of Judea to *Syria Palaestina* (whence the name Palestine).

The Temple Mount in the Byzantine Period (324–638 CE)

Emperor Constantine the First gained control of the Roman Empire in 324 CE and moved its capital from Rome to the Greek city of Byzantium which he renamed Constantinople. This, together with his declaring Christianity as the official religion of the empire, brought about a seismic shift in the area. The emperor and his mother, Queen Helena, consecrated sites in the Holy Land associated with the life of Jesus. In Jerusalem, the church of the Holy Sepulchre was built on the site assumed to have been the burial place of Christ. It was the first time during Jerusalem's long history that the focus of the city was shifted away from the Temple Mount to this newly built church, effectively denying any Jewish connection with the city.

There was a brief reversal of the triumph of Christianity during the reign of Constantine's nephew, Julian (361–363). Known as the Apostate, he was repelled by what he saw as Christianity's persecution of other religions. He favored the practice of paganism, with himself as *pontifex maximus*. Allowing freedom of worship to all, he revoked the ban on the entry of Jews to Jerusalem. His granting the Jews permission to rebuild the Temple was intended as a slight to the Christians, who saw its destruction as the fulfillment of the words of Jesus in Matthew 24.2. Attempts were made to build on the Temple Mount, but a fire on the site brought construction to an end. A Hebrew inscription of the text of Isaiah 66.14 on the southern part of the Western Wall is thought to have been carved by a pilgrim carried away by the messianic fervor of the time.

Up until recently, it was thought that the Temple Mount lay desolate for the remainder of the Byzantine period and was used as the city's garbage dump. However, the reported finding of part of a mosaic floor under the al-Aqsa Mosque in excavations carried out here in the 1930s (the only time that such activity was allowed on the Mount), points to the possible existence of houses at the southern part of the Mount during the Byzantine period. Regrettably, the limited finds make it impossible to draw any firm conclusions as to the extent of the built-up area.

The end of the Byzantine period in Jerusalem was heralded by the Persian invasion of 614 CE and completed by the Muslim conquest twenty-four years later.

The Temple Mount in the Byzantine period.

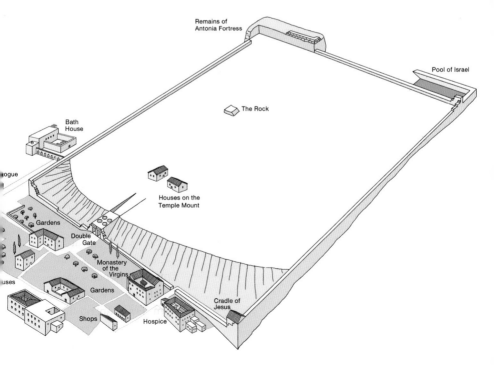

Remains of
Antonia Fortress

Pool of Israel

The Rock

Bath
House

ogue

Gardens

Double
Gate

Houses on the
Temple Mount

Monastery
of the
Virgins

uses

Gardens

Shops

Hospice

Cradle of
Jesus

The Temple Mount in the Early Muslim Period (638–1099)

The Caliph Omar, successor of Muhammad, the founder of the new religion Islam, accepted the city's surrender in 638 CE. Muslims regarded Jerusalem as a holy city and Jews were again granted the right to live there and pray on the Temple Mount. Some sources record that Omar ordered the site of the Temple Mount to be cleared of rubbish, thus exposing the Foundation Stone of the Jewish Temple. His plans for a "house of prayer" to be built on this site were delayed for some fifty years. At that time, the Umayyad dynasty, descendants of Omar who were based in Damascus, needed to divert support for a rival rebel dynasty based in Mecca. They opted for Jerusalem, which was under their jurisdiction. The grand design of the then Caliph Abd al-Malik was to build a magnificent center for Muslim pilgrimage on

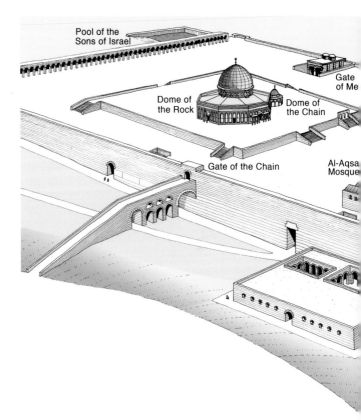

The Temple Mount in the Early Muslim period.

the Temple Mount, to be called the Dome of the Rock. Completed in 691 CE, it was neither a mosque nor a place of prayer, but a shrine to the Foundation Stone of the Temple. Modeled after Byzantine centrally designed commemorative churches, the Muslims transferred to the Temple Mount the story of the Night Journey of Muhammad from Mecca to the "farthest shrine" (*al-Aqsa*). From here they believed he ascended into Heaven. On completion of the Dome of the Rock, Caliph al-Walid built a mosque called al-Aqsa above the Southern Wall of the Temple Mount, on the former site of the Herodian Royal Stoa. The Temple Mount was known to the Muslims as *al-Haram al-Sharif* (The Noble Sanctuary). The reverence they accorded to the area assured the protection of the ancient

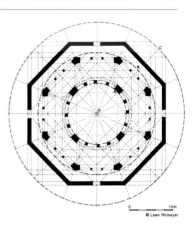

This geometric design shows how the walls, piers and pillars were set out from the inner and outer octagons that were formed by three concentric circles with a total radius of 100 feet (30.50 m).

Al-Haram al-Sharif

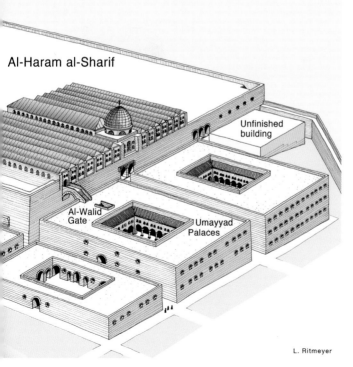

Unfinished building

Al-Walid Gate

Umayyad Palaces

L. Ritmeyer

Development of the Rock, from top to bottom:

1. The original shape of The Rock. The trapezoid depression in the centre was cut in the Muslim period to fix a pivot from which the circle of the inner dome was set out.

2. The cuttings in The Rock made by the Crusaders in preparation for its use as a high altar in the Dome of the Rock.

3. The Rock was covered by the Crusaders with slabs and stairways.

4. Reconstruction of the Crusader high altar built on The Rock.

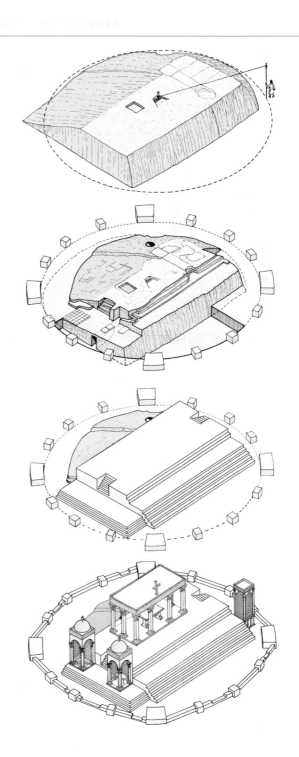

sites on the mount until the Crusaders set out from Europe to wrest Jerusalem from those whom they saw as infidels.

The Temple Mount in the Crusader Period (1099–1187)

The Foundation Stone or Rock (*Sakhra*) under the Dome of the Rock must have looked virtually the same to the Crusaders as it was left after 70 CE. Doubtless there must have been some weathering in the 600 years before it was roofed over by Abd al-Malik and it probably suffered some damage from falling debris. However, the fact that it had been all but ignored during the Roman period and willfully concealed during the era of the Byzantines, ensured, at least, that it was not mutilated. How different was the attitude of the Christian conquerors to that of the Muslims. An Arab historian wrote denouncing what the Crusaders had done:

> As for the Rock, the Franks built over it a church and altar, so that there was no longer any room for the hands that wished to seize the blessing from it or the eyes that longed to see it....The Rock, the object of pilgrimage, was hidden under constructions and submerged in all this sumptuous building.

This church into which the Dome of the Rock was converted was called *Templum Domini* (the Temple of the Lord) and the reason the Crusaders so defaced the Rock was their belief in the words of one Christian historian, that: "it disfigured the Temple of the Lord." The al-Aqsa at first served as a palace for the Crusader kings of Jerusalem and then as the headquarters of one of the Crusader orders, the Knights Templar. It was renamed *Templum Salomonis*, the Temple of Solomon. Many Crusader and Muslim shrines still dot the Temple Mount today and its appearance is essentially reminiscent of the Crusader period.

The Temple Mount in the Late Muslim Period (1187–1917)

After the battle of the Horns of Hattin in 1187, when the Ayyubid Sultan Saladin destroyed the Crusader army, the Muslims regained control of the Temple Mount. Saladin

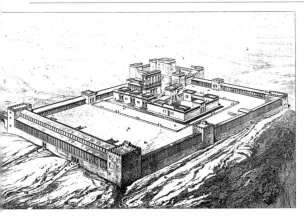

De Vogüé's reconstruction drawing of the Temple Mount, 1864.

Judith Montefiore

Lady Judith Montefiore and her husband Lord Moses, the Jewish philanthropist, were some of the first westerners not to have to resort to a disguise to enter the Temple Mount when they visited in the 1820s and 30s.

ordered the huge cross that crowned the Dome of the Rock to be torn down and reconsecrated the Mount as a Muslim sanctuary. Many of the beautifully wrought Crusader architectural elements were re-used. Apart from their practical and aesthetic value, their presence demonstrated the victory of Islam over Christianity. The marble slabs covering the Rock were removed and replaced by a wooden screen for protection.

Control of Jerusalem passed from the Ayyubid dynasty to the Mamluks and then to the Ottoman Turks. Throughout these years, the city stagnated, becoming a political backwater, but once it became a focus for Muslim pilgrimage, it developed its own characteristic architectural style. Numerous *madrasas*, or institutions for religious learning, and hostels were built in the area of the Temple Mount during the Mamluk period.

The Ottoman Turk, Suleiman the Magnificent, is famous for having rebuilt the walls of Jerusalem. He is also reputed to have sealed the Golden Gate to the Temple Mount. It has been suggested that the reason for this was to prevent the Christian Messiah from entering the city by this gate. Suleiman extensively renovated the religious buildings on the Mount, including the Dome of the Rock, where the date of this refurbishment can still be seen inscribed on the windows of the shrine.

During this period, access to the Temple Mount was forbidden to non-Muslims, although a handful of Europeans entered in disguise. In 1838, the American biblical scholar Edward Robinson, known as the "Father of Biblical Geography", discovered the spring of an arch protruding from the Western Wall of the Temple Mount, now named after him. Robinson's Arch turned out to be part of a monumental stairway that originally led up to Herod's Temple Mount. Another feature you will encounter on your tour is Barclay's

Gate in the Western Wall. It is named after the American missionary James Barclay, who discovered it from inside the platform while working as assistant to a Turkish architect doing repair work of the Dome of the Rock.

Restrictions on entering the Temple Mount were eased during the first half of the nineteeth century. The first real scientific work on the Mount was done by the French scholar and diplomat Count Melchior de Vogüé, whose 1864 publication contained a surprisingly accurate reconstruction drawing of the Temple Mount. In 1865, the following year, the British engineer Captain Charles Wilson mapped the Temple Mount for the first time as part of the British Ordnance Survey. The establishment of the Palestine Exploration Fund in the same year by a group of academics and clergymen was the major impetus to scientific investigation of the Mount. It was under their auspices that Wilson's colleague, Captain Charles Warren, carried out landmark explorations around the Mount for three years, from 1867 to 1870. Forbidden to dig inside the platform, Warren cut deep shafts alongside the walls, joining them up so that he could trace the bedrock contours of the Temple Mount and the subterranean courses of the walls. The set of plans resulting from these daring investigations and published in 1884 remain invaluable and are the basis for the plans in this guide book.

Another highlight in the history of Temple Mount research occurred in 1871, when a Greek inscription prohibiting the entrance of Gentiles into the Temple court found "north of the Temple Mount" was published by the French epigrapher and diplomat Charles Clermont-Ganneau (a fragment of an almost identical inscription was found near the Lions' Gate in 1935). The 1911 Parker Mission, in which a misguided English aristocrat caused havoc searching for Temple treasures, eventually digging inside the Dome of the Rock itself, resulted in the Muslim authorities banning all scientific exploration on the platform. This situation persisted through the period of the British Mandate (1919–1948) during which Muslims continued to control the Haram (The Noble Sanctuary). One exception to this rule was the archaeological excavation of R. W. Hamilton, director of the British Mandatory Department of Antiquities, who dug under

Captain (later Sir) Charles Warren

The daring nineteenth-century engineer who more than any other individual opened up the exploration of the Temple Mount. John "Rob Roy" MacGregor who canoed down the River Jordan in 1869 and visited Warren during his exploration work, wrote this about him: "Mr. Warren, indeed, seems to have a subterranean turn of mind, and it is fortunate when one's duty and inclination are both in the same direction."

Moshe Dayan

In 1967, shortly after the Six-Day War, Moshe Dayan ordered the Israeli flag removed from the Temple Mount and handed over the site of the Temple to the control of the Islamic Waqf as a gesture of peace. Jews were banned from holding prayer services there, but Israel retained security control of the area. (Photo: Israel Ministry of Defense)

the al-Aqsa Mosque in 1930 and discovered a mosaic floor dating from the Byzantine period.

The Temple Mount Today

Starting in 1961, when Jerusalem was under Jordanian rule and up to the Six-Day War, Dame Kathleen Kenyon, of the British School of Archaeology, excavated in the city. As part of her investigations, she carried out limited excavations to the south of the Temple Mount, but most of her work was concentrated in the City of David.

In 1967, Israel captured the Temple Mount from Jordan. Moshe Dayan, the then Israeli Defense Minister, established what has since been called "the status quo on the Temple Mount," with the Islamic Waqf, the Muslim Supreme Council, retaining custody of the Temple Mount, and overall security the responsibility of the State of Israel. Facts on the ground today, however, show that the Waqf exercises sovereignty, forbidding Jews to pray on the Mount. Independently, many rabbis issued rulings forbidding Jews from entering the Temple Mount for fear of unknowingly treading on the Holy of Holies and thus polluting the Mount.

Several Jewish activist groups challenge the Waqf's ban on worship and are exerting pressure for permission to pray openly on the Temple Mount. Various organizations deal with different aspects of the Temple. These include the Temple Mount Faithful, who strive to build the Third Temple in place of the Muslim shrines. The Temple Institute, based in the nearby Jewish Quarter, focuses on preparing ritual objects for use in this future temple. Although in the past, these groups worked independently, many of them are now cooperating and gaining adherents.

Fundamentalist Christians who believe that the building of the Third Temple is a necessary precondition for the Second Coming, support these efforts. An incident, highlighting the volatility of the site, occurred in 1969 when a young, disturbed Australian set fire to the al-Aqsa Mosque, causing serious riots. The mosque was soon restored and with it the usual mixture of quiet and tension.

With one exception, Israel never excavated on or under the Temple Mount but only alongside its walls or at some distance from the platform. The area near the southern end of the Western Wall and that to the south of the Southern Wall were excavated under the direction of Prof. Benjamin Mazar on behalf of the Israel Exploration Society and the Hebrew University of Jerusalem between 1968 and 1978. Prior to the Six-Day War, the prayer area of the Western Wall consisted of a narrow lane facing the Moroccan Quarter which was demolished and replaced by a paved plaza for worship and public gatherings. In 1968, the Religious Affairs Ministry began to excavate an underground tunnel to expose the full length of the Western Wall in a northerly direction. The sole occasion that investigation under the Mount took place was in 1981 when Rabbi Yehuda Getz, the rabbi of the Western Wall, cleared what is known as either Cistern 30 or Warren's Gate searching for Temple treasures. Excavation of the paved street along the Western Wall, part of Mazar's Temple Mount Excavations, resumed in the 1990s under the direction of Ronny Reich. In 1996, work to allow an exit to the *Via Dolorosa* from the Western Wall Tunnel and the Rock-hewn Aqueduct once more provoked serious hostilities. Also in 1996, the Waqf converted "Solomon's Stables" and the Triple Gate passageway into a large mosque, known as *al-Marwani*. A huge hole was dug in the surface of the Temple esplanade in order to build a wide staircase down to this mosque. Thousands of tons of soil were dumped into the Kedron Valley, without any archaeological supervision. In response to this illegal operation Israeli archaeologists set up the Temple Mount Sifting Project, which tries to systematically examine the rubble and salvage whatever possible.

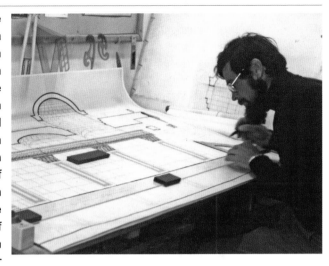

Leen in the architect's office of the Temple Mount Excavations, conducted between 1968 and 1978, drawing plans and sections of the Golden Gate.

Prof. Benjamin Mazar discussing with Kathleen the area she supervised during the Temple Mount Excavations.

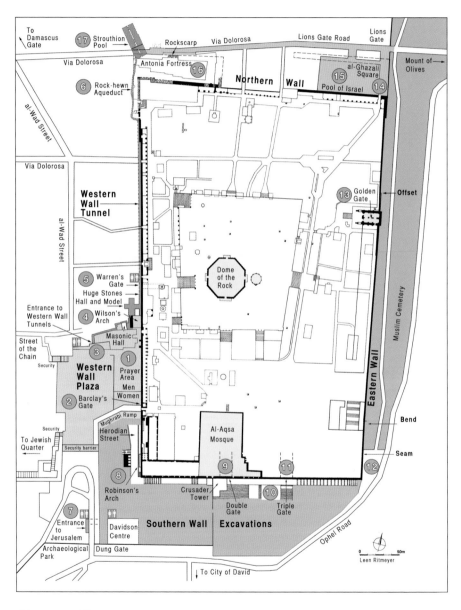

To
Damascus
Gate

17 Strouthion
Pool

Rockscarp

Via Dolorosa

Lions Gate Road

Lions
Gate

Via Dolorosa

Antonia Fortress

16

Northern   Wall

al-Ghazali
Square

15

Mount of
Olives

6 Rock-hewn
Aqueduct

Pool of Israel

14

al-Wad Street

Via Dolorosa

Western
Wall
Tunnel

13 Golden
Gate

Offset

al-Wad Street

Dome
of the
Rock

Muslim Cemetery

5 Warren's
Gate

Huge Stones
Hall and Model

Entrance to
Western Wall
Tunnels

4 Wilson's
Arch

Masonic
Hall

3

Street
of the
Chain

Security

1 Prayer
Area
Men

Western
Wall
Plaza

Women

2 Barclay's
Gate

Eastern Wall

Bend

Security

Mughrabi Ramp

Seam

To Jewish
Quarter

Herodian
Street

Security barrier

Al-Aqsa
Mosque

12

8

Robinson's
Arch

9

11

Crusader
Tower

Double
Gate

10

Triple
Gate

7

Entrance
to
Jerusalem

Davidson
Centre

Southern Wall   Excavations

Archaeological
Park

Dung Gate

Ophel Road

0   50m

Leen Ritmeyer

↓ To City of David

*A tour around the
Temple Mount walls.*

CHAPTER 2

A Walk Around the Temple Mount Walls

THE WESTERN WALL—EXPERIENCE THE WALL AT THE HEART OF JERUSALEM

In her famous "Jerusalem of Gold", Naomi Shemer sang of the wall at the heart of the city. Here, as nowhere else, you will feel the pulse of this sacred place and understand how everyone becomes a pilgrim when standing before these stones.

Useful Information

Entrance to the Western Wall Plaza is free and open to all, year-round, 24 hours a day. There are security checks at the entrances from the Dung Gate, the Jewish Quarter and the Street of the Chain.

The prayer area in front of the Wall is divided into a southern section for women and a larger northern area for men. Modest dress is required. Men must wear a head covering (a free skullcap can be picked up in the men's section).

The site is especially busy on Friday evenings when *Kabbalat Shabbat* (the arrival of the Sabbath) is celebrated. This occasion provides a unique opportunity to observe the different religious traditions and attire of various Jewish groups and to see their singing and dancing. The Wall is also a popular place for *Bar Mitzvahs*, which take place on Monday and Thursday mornings and on *Rosh Chodesh* (the first day of the Jewish month).

On Saturdays and festivals, smoking, photography and the use of mobile/cell phones are not allowed.

Tour

We shall begin our tour of the Temple Mount at the Western Wall, a first stop for almost every visitor to Jerusalem. The holiest spot in the world for the Jewish people, it owes its sanctity to the belief that it is the only remnant of the Jewish temple to have survived the destruction by Titus in 70 CE.

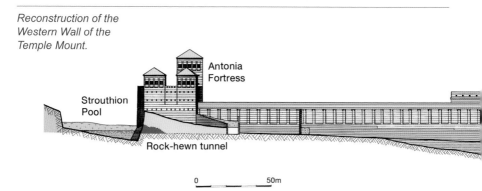

Reconstruction of the
Western Wall of the
Temple Mount.

Antonia Fortress

Strouthion Pool

Rock-hewn tunnel

0   50m

Always referred to as the Western Wall in Hebrew, it became known as the Wailing Wall by Gentiles who observed the tears shed by the people of Israel who came there to pray. Capturing the wall from the Jordanians was the climax of the Six-Day War and a historical turning point for Israelis and Jews worldwide. It has become such a symbol of hope that people of all religions tuck prayers and supplications written on slips of paper into the crevices between its stones.

A first visit to the Western Wall should be leisurely with enough time to take in the strong emotions that the site evokes. Prayer here is fervent, with the plaza used as an open-air synagogue. In contemplation, it is easy to understand the belief that the Divine Presence (*Shekhinah*) never leaves this place and that the words of the Song of Songs 2.9, "Behold, He (God) stands behind our wall (Hebrew, *Kotel*)," refer to this monumental piece of masonry.

1. Prayer Area

The narrow alley in front of the wall has been a place of Jewish prayer for centuries. From 1948 to 1967, during the nineteen years of Jordanian rule of the city, the only way to see the wall from Israel was to stand on Mount Zion and view it from afar. With the reunification of Jerusalem, the wall soon became a national and religious shrine. One of the first Israeli actions was to bulldoze the partly-ruined Moroccan Quarter that stood in front of the wall and create the plaza which we see today.

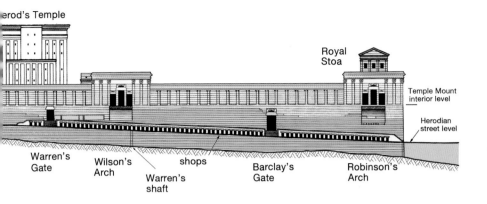

Contrary to tradition the Western Wall did not form part of Solomon's Temple, but is a section of the massive retaining walls built by Herod the Great to support the enormous amount of fill needed for his extension of the Temple platform. When building the plaza, the whole area was lowered, revealing further Herodian stone courses. These massive stones are typical of Herod the Great's building style and can easily be distinguished from the smaller stones higher in the wall that date from later periods. Herodian masonry is characterized by finely cut margins and flat bosses, finished with a fine pick. The stones were cut with such precision and fitted together so perfectly that no mortar was necessary.

The stones in the seven lowest courses in this part of the Western Wall belong to the retaining wall, 15 feet (5 m) wide, that Herod began building in 19 BCE. An additional twenty-one stone courses lie beneath the level of the present-day plaza. Here the wall's foundation course is, as elsewhere, built on bedrock 70 feet (21 m) below the pavement.

Above these stones are four courses of large stones laid in the Umayyad period (around 700 CE). Both types of masonry are so strong and well built that, so far, no earthquake has damaged these walls. The big earthquake of 1927 caused the destruction of the al-Aqsa Mosque, but not even a crack appeared in the Herodian masonry! The upper third of the Western Wall is made up of small stones that started to crumble in 2008. This upper part of the wall could date from any time after the Early Muslim period. The major part,

What happens to the prayer notes?

Twice a year, the notes are removed by the Rabbi of the Western Wall and his team in order to make room for further prayer requests. The removed papers also include many that have been sent from all over the world, addressed simply to God, Jerusalem. As according to Jewish religious practice, no piece of writing that contains the name of God should be discarded, the notes are then buried on the Mount of Olives.

Ayyubid-Mamluk masonry

Umayyad masonry

Herodian masonry

The Western Wall Plaza today, indicating the different courses of masonry through the ages.

however, was built in the Mamluk period (1250–1517) as the supporting wall for the west portico.

The original length of the Western Wall was 1,590 feet (485 m) and Josephus tells us that it had four gates. The remains of two of these can be accessed from the plaza, Barclay's Gate and Wilson's Arch. There was an entrance above Wilson's Arch. This arch, named after the nineteenth-century explorer, Charles Wilson, lies on the left side of the Western Wall Plaza, the side reserved for men's prayers. However, there is a special entrance for both men and women into this area as part of the tour of the Western Wall Tunnels. Most scholars agree that the present-day arch dates from the Umayyad period, and that it was a restoration of the original Herodian arch that was part of a bridge that gave access to the Temple Mount in the time of Herod.

2. Barclay's Gate

Named after Dr. James Barclay, the nineteenth-century American missionary who discovered it, Barclay's Gate is lo-

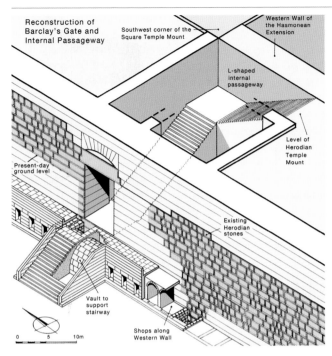

Reconstruction of
Barclay's Gate and
Internal Passageway

Southwest corner of the
Square Temple Mount

Western Wall of
the Hasmonean
Extension

L-shaped
internal
passageway

Level of
Herodian
Temple
Mount

Present-day
ground level

Existing
Herodian
stones

Vault to
support
stairway

Shops along
Western Wall

0   5   10m

*A cutaway
reconstruction
drawing of Barclay's
Gate and internal
passageway.*

*(below left) The lintel
of Barclay's Gate
(outlined in black),
located in the right-
hand corner of the
Western Wall Plaza.*

*(below right) View of
the lintel from inside
the women's prayer
chamber. (Photo:
Clare Ritmeyer)*

cated on the right of the plaza in the women's prayer section. The massive lintel of this gate is visible just above the steps that lead into a small chamber beneath the bridge to the Temple Mount. As this chamber is in the area reserved for women, male visitors will have to rely on female witnesses to describe the interi-

or, where the central section of the lintel can be seen. Behind this lintel, parts of the original Herodian L-shaped stepped passageway have been preserved.   Below the sill of the gate, Warren discovered the spring of an arch that, in the Herodian period, supported a stairway leading up

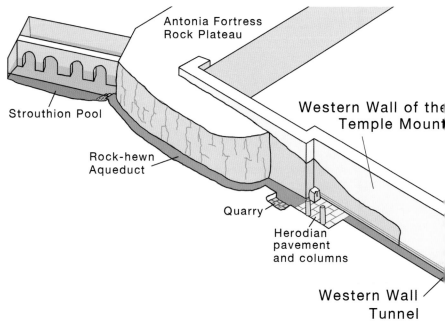

Antonia Fortress
Rock Plateau

Strouthion Pool

Western Wall of the
Temple Mount

Rock-hewn
Aqueduct

Quarry

Herodian
pavement
and columns

Western Wall
Tunnel

from the main street to the gate.

3. Entrance to the Western Wall Tunnels

The exposed section at the Western Wall Plaza is almost 190 feet (60 m) long. At the northern side of the plaza is an entrance to the Western Wall Tunnels, which allows access to an additional 787 feet (240 m) of Herod's retaining wall. After the 1967 Six-Day War, the Israeli Ministry of Religious Affairs began excavations to expose its northern extension, digging beneath the Muslim Quarter. Through these tunnels you can walk alongside the wall as far as the Antonia Fortress and exit onto the *Via Dolorosa*. The area is now controlled by the Western Wall Heritage Foundation.

THE WESTERN WALL TUNNELS—FOLLOW THE WALL HIDDEN IN DARKNESS

Having felt the emotional impact of the Western Wall, you will be pleased to know that you can follow this wall deep underground for a considerable distance in a northerly direction.

Useful Information

Access to the site is only by guided tours that must be reserved ahead using the reservation hotline: +972 2 6271333, or booking online at http://english.thekotel.org/VisitorInfo.asp?id=1. The website recommends that you book two months in advance.

Visiting hours: Sunday–Thursday: 7 a.m.–evening (depending on reservations);
     Fridays and eve of Jewish holidays: 7 a.m.–12 p.m.

Entrance fee (payable when booking). To receive ticket, you must bring the credit card with which your reservation was made.

Tour lasts approximately 75 minutes.

Closed on Saturdays and Jewish festivals, and on the eves of *Rosh Hashana*, *Yom Kippur*, and *Tisha B'av* (the Ninth of Av).

One enters a long and narrow tunnel that was called the "Secret Passage" by Charles Warren who discovered

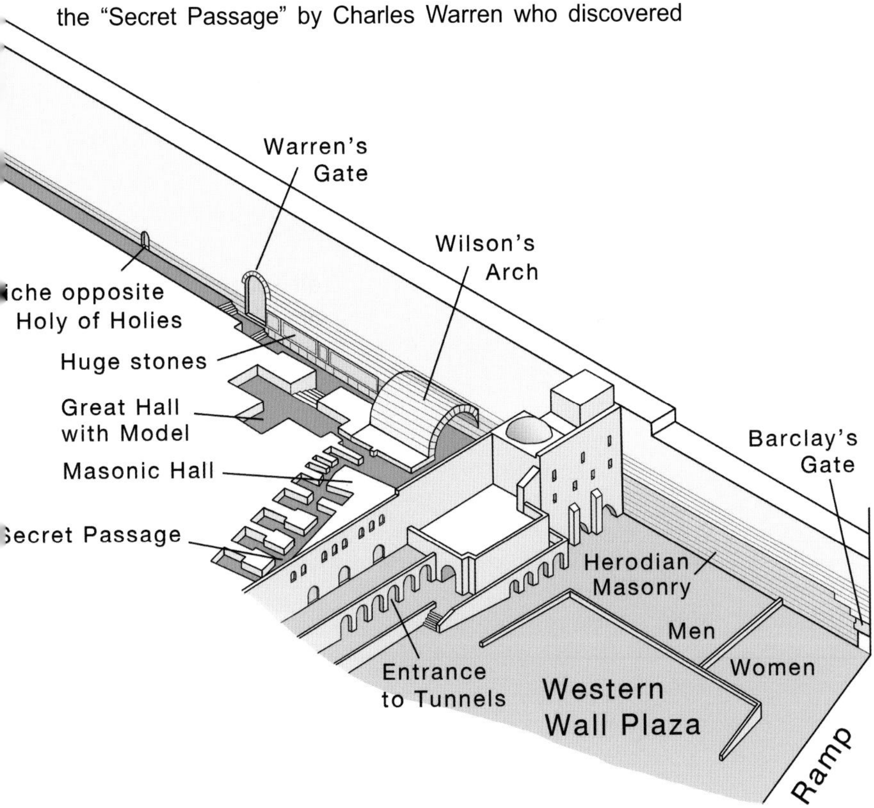

Plan of Western Wall Tunnels.

it in the 1860s. The adjacent two-story-high vaulting was constructed after the destruction of 70 CE, possibly in the Roman or Early Muslim periods. This construction follows the line of the original bridge that was built by Herod the Great and ended at Wilson's Arch.

4. Wilson's Arch and the Masonic Hall

Before reaching Wilson's Arch, we see one of the lower vaulted rooms called the Large Hall or Hasmonean Hall. It was dubbed the "Masonic Hall" by Warren, because of an association with the Freemasons at the time of its discovery and displays high standards of architecture. The walls are built of plain dressed stone and feature decorative pilasters that were crowned with Corinthian capitals. Only one interior corner capital has survived. Entrance to the hall was through a double doorway. The hall is thought to date from the late Hasmonean or early Herodian period and may have served as a type of municipal office. Some scholars have identified it with the Council Chamber mentioned by Josephus in *War* 5.144 as standing near the "western portico of the temple."

Reconstruction of the Masonic Hall, or Hall of the Freemasons.

Wilson's Arch can be viewed from a platform that is accessible to all visitors, including women, who are otherwise

barred from this section of the Western Wall Plaza. The
original arch was the first in a series of arches that formed
a bridge spanning the Tyropoeon Valley below. It linked the
Temple Mount with the Upper City, where the Hasmonean

Wilson's Arch.

*The Masonic Hall
today.*

Stone quarrying

A stone cutter (right) cuts channels in the rock, while another worker pours water over logs that have been hammered into the grooves. The pressure of the swelling wood causes the block to split off from the bedrock.

Palace was located and where most of the priestly families lived. It is therefore also known as the Bridge of the Priests. This bridge supported an aqueduct bringing water from the "Solomon's Pools" near Bethlehem to a huge cistern on the Temple Mount, known as the "Great Sea."

5. Great Hall and Warren's Gate

North of the latter area is a large cruciform hall, where a multi-level model is used to explain the history of Jerusalem and the Temple Mount. Through one of the branches of this hall, one gets a first glimpse of four of the largest stones placed by Herod the Great in the Herodian Western Wall.

These stones are truly enormous. Going down a stairway, one is confronted with the largest of the four ashlars, which is 44 feet 2 inches (13.45 m) long, over 10 feet (3.20 m) high and, according to ground-penetrating radar tests, from 6 to 8 feet or 1.8 to 2.5 m deep. If this is so, then this stone weighs about 200 tons. The other ashlars are, respectively, 6 feet 7 inches (2 m), 39 feet 8 inches (12.10 m) and 16 feet 7 inches

The largest of the enormous Herodian ashlars visible in the Western Wall Tunnel. The stone begins at the margin on the left and ends in the far distance where the person is standing, making it longer than a modern bus.

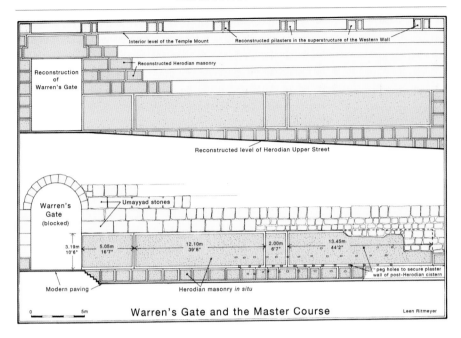

Interior level of the Temple Mount   Reconstructed pilasters in the superstructure of the Western Wall

Reconstructed Herodian masonry

Reconstruction
of
Warren's Gate

Reconstructed level of Herodian Upper Street

Warren's
Gate
(blocked)

Umayyad stones

3.19m
10'6"   5.05m
16'7"   12.10m
39'8"   2.00m
6'7"   13.45m
44'2"

peg holes to secure plaster
wall of post-Herodian cistern

Modern paving   Herodian masonry *in situ*

0   5m

Warren's Gate and the Master Course

Leen Ritmeyer

(5.05 m) long. There are another 15 stone courses below this huge course where the wall rests on bedrock. So, why did Herod put these huge stones so high up in the wall? He probably put them at the upper street level, so that everyone passing by would be duly impressed by his architectural and engineering skills! This stone course is called the Master Course, a term borrowed from the Southern Wall Excavations where a huge stone course is located between the Double

Warren's Gate and the "Master Course". Below are the remains in situ *and above is a suggested reconstruction.*

Moving the stones.
A stone mason (lower left) dresses a rough block, leaving projections for lifting. Using a short tripod crane, the stones are lifted onto wooden rollers to be pulled by teams of oxen to the building site.

Gate and the southeast corner of the Temple Mount.

As mentioned above, Josephus recorded four gates in the Western Wall of the Temple Mount. So far, we have viewed two of them, Wilson's Arch and Barclay's Gate. Next to the enormous ashlars are the remains of the gate that was closest to the Temple, i.e., Warren's Gate, named after Charles Warren. The gate opening is located between the northern edge of the last of these mammoth stones and the continuation of the Herodian stones in the Western Wall about 16 feet (5 m) farther on. This Herodian gate led to an underground passageway, similar to that of Barclay's Gate, which was L-shaped with a stairway to the Temple Mount. The arch above Warren's Gate is of a later period, probably Early Muslim. In the Crusader period, this passage was blocked and the interior space used as a water cistern (see the *Sabil Qaytbay* on the Tour of the Temple Mount Platform).

In 1981, while removing debris from the tunnel, Meir Yehuda Getz, Rabbi of the Western Wall, covertly entered the underground passage behind Warren's Gate and began tunneling towards the Dome of the Rock. It is generally believed by orthodox Jews that the Ark of the Covenant is located in a secret chamber below the Dome of the Rock. After a fruitless search, however, the tunnelers were exposed and the gate was blocked up by a massive concrete wall. Subsequently the surface of this concrete wall was chipped to give it the appearance of an ancient fill; the smooth concrete drew too many questions from visitors.

Just beyond this ancient gate, a small arched niche in the wall is said to be located directly opposite the Foundation Stone—"The Rock"—inside the Dome of the Rock where the Holy of Holies of Solomon's Temple stood. People can often be seen praying here.

Continuing north, the narrow tunnel follows the stone courses of the Herodian Western Wall for quite some distance. Towards the end of the straight tunnel the Western Wall is cut out of the rock, above street level. The rock here has been carved to look like Herodian stones. A large unfinished block of quarry rock can be seen near the Herodian pavement and two nearby columns appear to have formed part of a

Where is the Ark of the Covenant?

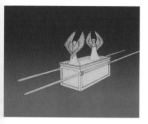

From the biblical record it appears that the Ark remained in the Holy of Holies of Solomon's Temple until the reign of King Manasseh who set a graven image in the Temple (2 Kings 21.7; 2 Chr 33.7). Following its restoration by Josiah in 2 Chronicles 35.3, we hear no more of the whereabouts of the Ark in the Scriptures and it does not appear on the Arch of Titus in Rome which depicts the triumphant procession of the Romans with the spoils of the Jerusalem Temple after its destruction in 70 CE. Theories abound as to where it might be found ranging from Mount Nebo, east of the Jordan River (based on a reference in 2 Maccabees 2.1–8) to Axum in Ethiopia.

The Rock-hewn Aqueduct in the Western Wall Tunnel.

series of shops that were built alongside this street. From this point onwards, the Western Wall disappears and the tunnel continues a few meters distant from the wall because here, at the northwest corner of the Temple Mount, was the Antonia Fortress. The rocky area between the tunnel and the Western Wall may have been the base for a street leading up to the fortress.

6. The Rock-hewn Aqueduct

The tunnel now continues into a Rock-hewn Aqueduct that predates the Herodian Temple Mount. Although labeled as

The double-vaulted Strouthion Pool.

Hasmonean it is probably earlier, based on other similar aqueducts, such as the one in Gibeon from the First Temple period. It ends in a large double-vaulted pool, the Strouthion Pool, that in Herodian times was open to the sky and used as a water reservoir for the Antonia Fortress. The Romans covered the reservoir with a double vault in the second century CE. The continuation of this pool can be seen in the Convent of the Sisters of Zion on the *Via Dolorosa* (see Tour of Northern Wall, p. 91).

TIP: After completing your explorations of this side of the Temple Mount, we recommend, if time allows, leaving the other sections of the Temple Mount tour for another day. You could then return and start afresh at the Southern Wall Excavations and do as many more sections of the tour as you wish. You could, of course, continue to the northeast corner of the Temple Mount and follow the Northern Wall at this juncture, but the suggested tour presents the information in a more logical sequence.

Before we enter the sacred compound of the Temple Mount, let us walk around the remaining outer walls that support this massive complex, the Southern, Eastern and Northern Walls.

7. Entrance to the Jerusalem Archaeological Park—Davidson Centre

After the Six-Day War, systematic excavations were carried out near the southern end of the Western Wall and around the Southern Wall. These were directed by Prof. Benjamin Mazar and continued for 10 years. Ronny Reich reopened excavations in this area in the 1990s in the framework of the development of the Jerusalem Archaeological Park.

The Davidson Centre, at the entrance to the park, exhibits the history of the Temple using state-of-the-art technology. A virtual reality reconstruction of Herod's Temple is the highlight of the center.

JERUSALEM ARCHAEOLOGICAL PARK—DAVIDSON CENTRE: WALK IN THE PARK AROUND THE SOUTHERN WALL

Israeli archaeologists have created a peaceful park around the Southern Wall of Herod's Temple Mount. Of all the tours suggested in this guide book, this is the section that affords the visitor the best opportunity to examine remains from the time when the Temple was at the heart of Jerusalem.

> **Useful Information**
>
> Visiting Hours:
> Sunday–Thursday: 8 a.m.–5 p.m.
> Fridays: 8 a.m.–2 p.m.
> Closed on Saturdays and Jewish holidays.
> Entrance fee.
> Guided tours of the park and the model must be booked in advance by telephoning:
> +972 2 6277550. For more information go to www.archpark.org.il.

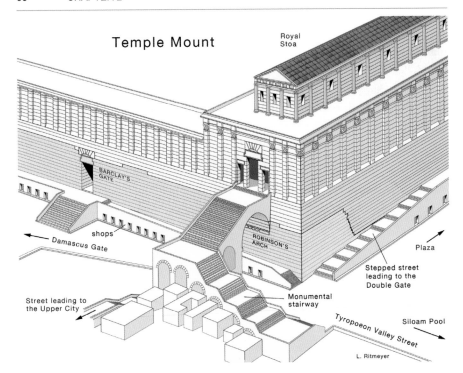

Temple Mount

Royal Stoa

BARCLAY'S GATE

shops

ROBINSON'S ARCH

Damascus Gate

Plaza

Street leading to the Upper City

Stepped street leading to the Double Gate

Monumental stairway

Tyropoeon Valley Street

Siloam Pool

L. Ritmeyer

Reconstruction of Robinson's Arch at the southwest corner of the Temple Mount.

Remains of Robinson's Arch.

8. Robinson's Arch

The southernmost gate in the Western Wall of Herod's Temple Mount was located over what is known today as Robinson's Arch, named after its discoverer, the American biblical scholar, Edward Robinson. The spring of this arch, which looks like some projecting stones, can be seen in the wall near the southwest corner of the Temple Mount. These arch stones rest on a row of blocks with margins and bosses, known as imposts (the eleventh course above the level of the paved street below). The excavations directed by Benjamin Mazar revealed a series of equidistant arches of graduated height, ascending from the south and then turning eastwards over Robinson's Arch. After several theories were put forward, it was concluded that these are the remains of a monumental stairway that led down from

The stepped street next to and north of the pier of Robinson's Arch that, according to Josephus, went "up again to the hill" (Ant. 15.410).

the Royal Portico to the street in the Tyropoeon Valley.

This construction has been described accurately by Josephus: "The last [gate] led to the other part of the city, from which it was separated by many steps going down to the ravine and from here up again to the hill" (*Ant.* 15.410). The phrase "up again to the hill" refers to the narrow street found adjacent to the northern part of the pier that supported Robinson's Arch and which led to the Upper City. This ascending street was built over arches, the remains of which are still visible. There are four openings in the pier (supporting wall) of the massive arch. The finds here show that they were probably shops which served the multitudes who converged on this area.

Trumpeting Stone

On the pavement near the southwest corner, a parapet

(above) Reconstruction drawing of a priest blowing the trumpet in the recess above which was inscribed "to the place of trumpeting to [announce]..." and (left) the trumpeting stone inscription.

fragment was found, bearing an incomplete inscription above a recess. The inscription reads, "*l'bet hatqia l'hakh…*," which most scholars have suggested completing to read, "To the place of trumpeting to [announce]." It appears that the top of this corner of the Temple Mount was the designated place described by Josephus (*War* 4.582) where the priest used to announce the beginning or end of the sabbath with a trumpet blast. The trumpet used was probably a silver trumpet like the one mentioned in Numbers 10.2 and depicted on the Arch of Titus in Rome, which portrays the capture of the Temple treasures by the Romans. The original inscription is now in the Israel Museum. A facsimile was put in its place on the parapet stone and moved from the place where it was found to a more accessible location a few meters away, but still close to the southwest corner.

Tyropoeon Valley Street

Looking north, we see a large section of a beautifully preserved Herodian pavement, with the curbstones bordering both sides still clearly visible. This street ran along the Western Wall beginning at the present-day Damascus Gate. It passed through the Tyropoeon Valley, going under Robinson's Arch and terminated at the southern city gate. A branch of this major thoroughfare descended by steps to the Siloam Pool, located near the latter gate. A large drain runs below this street, which can be traversed from the Siloam Pool up to Robinson's Arch. Don't be surprised to see people exiting from a fenced opening in the pavement. They have walked underground from the City of David (one-way only) and can continue touring in the Archaeological Park. In 70 CE many Jerusalemites tried to escape through this same tunnel, but were cruelly killed by the Romans when they were discovered.

View of the Herodian drain with its vaulted ceiling beneath the street below Robinson's Arch. The original flat-roofed drain was rerouted after it was cut by the construction of the Herodian southwest corner. (Photo: Alexander Schick)

The drain beneath the street in the Tyropoeon Valley has flat cover stones and may pre-date the Herodian vaulted section.

These pilaster stones, found amidst the fallen debris on the street, originate from the Western Portico of the Temple Mount.

Shops that were built against the Western Wall and the aforementioned shops on the opposite side of the street, gave this major north-south thoroughfare the distinctive character of a market street. The Western Wall was much higher in the Herodian period than now. The many fallen stones seen lying on the street came from the Western Portico that was destroyed by the Romans. In the destruction layers, pilaster stones were found, similar to those that have been preserved intact at another Herodian structure,

Pilasters in the outer walls of the Tomb of the Patriarchs in Hebron.

the Tomb of the Patriarchs in Hebron. Remains of pilasters have also been found at the enclosure of nearby Mamre, where Herodian masonry is also in evidence. In both cases, the pilaster construction began at the level of the inner court. From these parallels we deduce that the walls of the Temple Mount were of a similar construction.

Inscription of Isaiah 66.14

An intriguing feature of the Western Wall can be seen if you stand on the Herodian street with your back to the pier and the four shops and look up. Four courses below the impost blocks of Robinson's Arch there is a groove that carried a water pipe in the Byzantine period. It is, however, in a stone just to the left of center of the course below this that the feature is visible.

The margin of this Herodian stone frames a carved inscription which reads in Hebrew: "*Ur'item ve sas libchem va atzmotam ka deshe,*" which is a quote from the prophet Isaiah 66.14: "And when ye see this, your heart shall rejoice and your bones shall flourish like an herb." In the inscription however, "your bones" is changed to "their bones" and the words "shall flourish" are missing. It would in fact appear that

The Isaiah 66.14 inscription is located five courses below Robinson's Arch, underneath the Byzantine groove.

Stone inscription citing Isaiah 66.14, discovered in the Western Wall below Robinson's Arch.

the graffiti artist was under pressure and unable to complete the quote.

This carving was one of the most dramatic and memorable finds of the excavations that followed the Six-Day War. According to Professor Mazar, it probably dates from the fourth century when the Emperor Julian the Apostate gave permission to the Jews to rebuild the Temple. The carving was seen as an expression of a people who had returned to the Land full of hope to restore the ritual that was the focus of their lives. Their hopes were apparently dashed in 363 CE, when disasters such as earthquakes and fires at the building site of the Temple brought the project to an end.

Southwest Corner

Standing in this area during the Herodian period, you would have found yourself at a busy intersection of the city. There would be people converging from five different directions: from the monumental stairway over Robinson's Arch, from the Upper Market which was located under the narrow street

The header and stretcher construction at the southwest corner of the Temple Mount. The stones are laid alternately facing west and south.

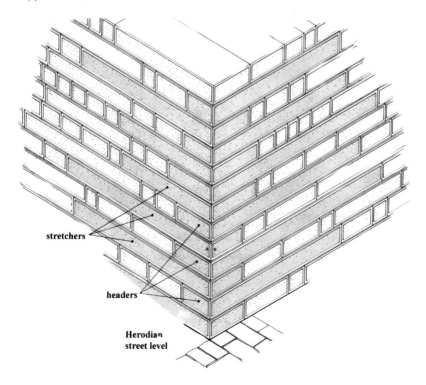

stretchers

headers

Herodian
street level

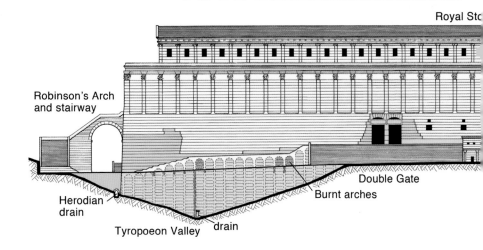

Royal Sto

Robinson's Arch and stairway

Double Gate

Burnt arches

Herodian drain

Tyropoeon Valley drain

that ran along the Western Wall and from the main Tyropoeon Valley Street. From the right (east), they came either from another narrow street that skirted the Southern Wall or from the massive plaza that lay to the south of the Temple Mount. The southwest corner has survived to a considerable height due to the enormous corner stones built in alternate courses of headers (stones laid with their short side exposed) and stretchers (stones laid with their long side exposed). Some of these stones are 40 feet (12 m) long, over 3 feet 4 inches (1 m) high, 8 feet (2.5 m) wide and weigh over 75 tons. Even the Romans with all their engineering skills were not able to dislodge them. In fact, all four corners of the Herodian Temple Mount have been preserved to a great height.

THE SOUTHERN WALL

Rounding the corner, we look up to see the southern retaining wall of Herod's Temple Mount, which was 912 feet (278 m) long. The upper nine courses of the Herodian stones at the southwest corner continue to the east for some 75 feet (23 m), where an almost vertical break occurs. The Persians invaded the country in 614 and destroyed many Byzantine churches and monasteries as well as the wall section to the east of this break. A stepped Herodian street built against the Southern Wall ascends to the Double Gate, one of the

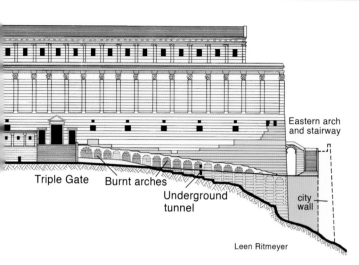

Reconstruction of the Southern Wall of Herod's Temple Mount.

Eastern arch and stairway

Triple Gate   Burnt arches

Underground tunnel

city wall

Leen Ritmeyer

two gates in this wall that date to the latter period.

We can view the remains of this magnificent gateway by passing through one of two openings in the Early Muslim wall that is perpendicular to the Southern Wall. The openings

The Southern Wall of the Temple Mount, with a view of the excavations at its southwest corner.

were created by the excavators during the 1970s.

9. Double Gate

The Double Gate is the westernmost of the two Herodian gates in the Southern Wall. From the outside only the blocked part of one gate can be seen. The other gate is open, but obscured from view by the large Crusader tower built in front.

The original lintel of the gate is visible behind the decorative arch that was applied on the exterior in the Umayyad period, when the Double Gate was again used to enter the Temple Mount. The decoration of this arch and the projecting

Reconstruction of the Double Gate and its underground passageway underneath the exquisitely decorated domes.

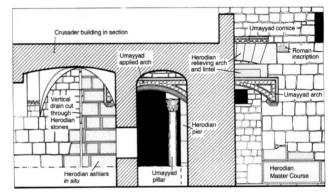

(above right) Elevation showing the remains of the Herodian Double Gate inside the Crusader building and (below) reconstruction of the Double Gate's exterior.

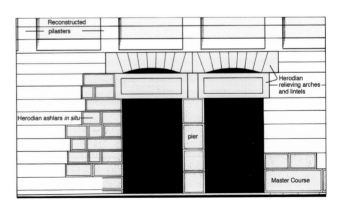

cornice above it are identical to the decoration on both the interior and exterior of the Golden Gate. The Double Gate led into a 240-foot- (73-m-) long passageway that ascended northwards, giving access to the Temple Court above. In the southern part of the passageway, four Herodian domes decorated with floral and geometric designs interwoven in intricate patterns have been preserved. One dome has a vine with bunches of grapes twined among eight squares arranged in an eight-pointed star. Another has a giant wreath made of rosettes arranged around a circular multi-petalled scallop with acanthus leaves in the corners. Amazingly, behind the Southern Wall, this gate, including the ceiling, has been preserved in its entirety!

Drawing of the northwest dome in the underground passageway of the Double Gate. (Drawing: Nathaniel Ritmeyer)

Monumental Stairway

Visitors may climb up a wide flight of steps to the Double Gate area. The thirty steps, partially rock-hewn and partly built of large stones conforming to the slope of the mountain, have been restored by the excavators. The total width

Reconstruction of the Double and Triple Gate area in the Herodian period.

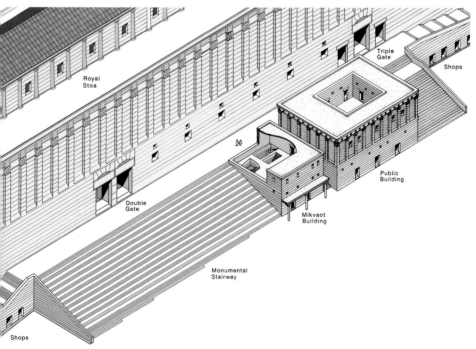

Royal Stoa

Triple Gate

Shops

Double Gate

Mikvaot Building

Public Building

Monumental Stairway

Shops

L. Ritmeyer

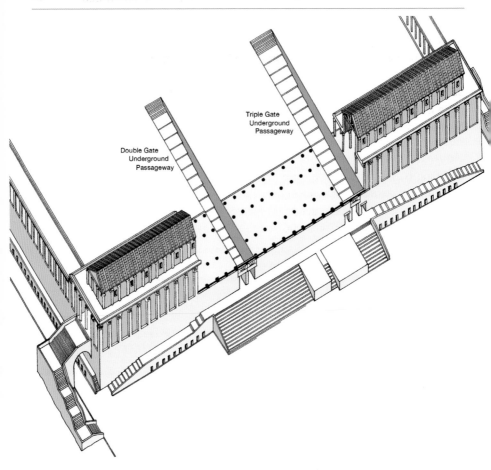

Double Gate
Underground
Passageway

Triple Gate
Underground
Passageway

Reconstruction of the Double and Triple Gate underground passageways.

found was approximately 105 feet (32 m), which represents only half the original width, based on a symmetrical layout of these steps to the longitudinal axis of the gate. The enormous dimensions of this monumental stairway suggest that it was the grandest of all the approaches to the Temple gates. It therefore was probably ascended by the majority of pilgrims going to worship in the Temple. Its alternate steps and landings ensure a reverent ascent.

Remains of a large paved plaza were found at the bottom of the steps. For reasons of town planning, such an expanse was necessary as a place of assembly. The dimensions of this plaza are comparable to those found in Athens and Priene.

It must have been an awesome experience for pilgrims to climb the magnificent stairway from this plaza to the Temple Mount and enter through the beautifully decorated underground passageway. For this reason it has been suggested that the Double Gate may have been the Beautiful Gate mentioned in Acts 3, where the lame man was healed by the Apostles Peter and John.

Royal Stoa

Standing on this plaza today, one looks up to the looming black dome of the al-Aqsa Mosque. During the Herodian period, the Royal Stoa graced the whole length of the Southern Wall. Constructed in the shape of a basilica with four rows of forty columns each, it had a central nave and

The Royal Stoa depicted with a pitched roof. As roof tiles had not yet been introduced at this time, the original roof was probably covered with metal plates made of copper or lead.

The Temple Mount Excavations, looking east toward the Mount of Olives cemetery. At left, the outline of the Triple Gate can be seen in the Southern Wall.

two aisles. The central apse in the east end was the place of meeting for the Sanhedrin, the supreme Jewish Council. The main part of this building was used for the changing of money and purchase of sacrificial animals.

It needs to be remembered that the Herodian additions to the original 500-cubit-square Temple Mount were not considered to be part of the sacred area. However, during the pilgrimage festivals to Jerusalem, such as Passover and the Feast of Tabernacles (*Sukkot*), some priests took advantage of their status to set up stalls in the inner courts of the Temple. So, when we read in the Gospels that Jesus drove away the money-changers and those who sold sacrificial animals, it would appear that this was an occasion when the market had spilled over from the Royal Stoa into the holy area, thus profaning it.

In this model, made by Alec Garrard, the stalls of the money-changers can be seen in the holy area.

10. Buildings between the Double and Triple Gates

To the east of the monumental stairway of the Double Gate are several *mikva'ot* (ritual baths) and reservoirs cut in the bedrock. The building that housed these baths for ritual purification was suitably located next to one of the main entrances to the Temple Mount.

Located to the east of these baths, a complex of rock-cut Herodian chambers were discovered that apparently belonged to a large public building. It has been suggested that this may have been one of the three council-houses mentioned in Mishnah *Sanhedrin* 11.2, "One [Council] used to sit at *the gate of the Temple Mount*, one used to sit at the gate of the Temple court and one used to sit in the Chamber of Hewn Stone."

The lowest course of stones between the Double Gate and the southeast corner is twice as high as the regular Herodian courses. This is the original "Master Course," after which the massive stones already encountered in the Western Wall Tunnels were named. These huge stones are positioned here in a place most likely to elicit the awe of passersby.

Three young men showing the large size of the first stone of the Master Course next to the Double Gate.

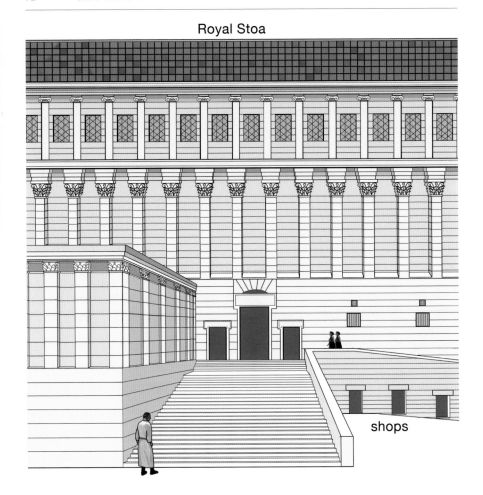

Royal Stoa

shops

Reconstruction of the Triple Gate and the stairway that leads up to it. Behind the gate entrance was an underground passageway, similar to that of the Double Gate.

11. Triple Gate

Of the original Herodian Triple Gate only the western jamb has been preserved. The present triple-arched gate, which dates from the Umayyad period, gave access to an underground passageway that led up to the Temple Mount. It also gave access to huge underground structures that are popularly known as Solomon's Stables and which in recent years have been converted into the *al-Marwani* Mosque. In the western wall of the underground passageway only the bottom part of one column, which once supported the Royal Stoa, has survived the Roman destruction of 70 CE.

Despite modern findings, many people refer to the

Double and Triple Gate as the Huldah Gates, mentioned in Mishnah *Middot*. This tractate, however, describes a pre-Herodian Temple Mount that later became an inner Temple Court after the Herodian expansion. The Huldah Gates therefore refer to the gates in the southern wall of the pre-Herodian Temple Mount, as the Herodian additions are completely ignored in the Mishnah. They were located some 240 feet (73 m) inside the Southern Wall.

View of the Herodian western doorjamb of the Triple Gate.

Stepped Street

The stepped street mentioned above ran the full length of the Southern Wall. It ascended from the southwest corner and was built over a series of shops until it reached the monumental stairway in front of the Double Gate. In between the two gates the street was level, descending again from the Triple Gate to the southeast corner. Here too it was built over arched cells that served as shops. Josephus tells us that in 70 CE the Roman soldiers, after burning the Temple, set other fires in this area (*War* 6.353–355). The scene

A burnt arch below the Triple Gate, evidence of a conflagration from the time of the Roman destruction of Jerusalem in 70 CE.

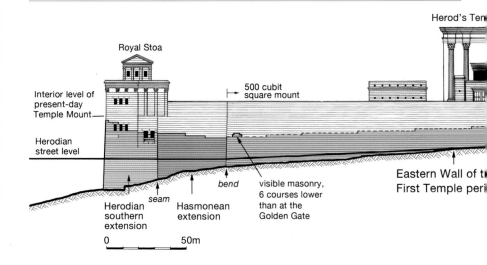

Reconstruction of the Eastern Wall of the Temple Mount.

comes vividly to life when we look down along the wall from the Triple Gate to the southeast corner. Here we see the unmistakable imprints of the vaults of these shops burnt into the wall—an eerie reminder of the awful inferno!

THE EASTERN WALL—DECIPHERING THE PUZZLE OF THE OLDEST OF THE TEMPLE MOUNT WALLS

Of all the walls of the Temple platform, this wall is the most difficult to understand. However, it amply repays close attention. In fact, if such wall remains as were discovered here were associated with the Western Wall, they would long ago have been lovingly encased with glass as a precious remnant of the original Mountain of the Lord.

Useful Information

Tourists are allowed to follow the path that runs parallel to the Eastern Wall as far as the Lions' Gate (St. Stephen's Gate). It is not, however, permitted to wander off this path to examine elements of the wall, and access to this area is forbidden during Muslim funerals as the path traverses their cemetery.

At this point, it would be helpful to get our bearings in regard to the original Temple platform. It was probably King Hezekiah who enlarged the then existing Temple Mount

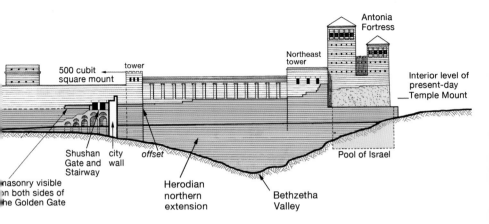

to a square compound, measuring 500 cubits (861 ft./ 262.5 m) each side. He also extended the city to accommodate the escapees from the Assyrian invasion of 722 BCE. Leen Ritmeyer pinpointed archaeological clues to the original platform by starting at one of the stairways that lead up to the platform of the Dome of the Rock, which we have not yet visited. By following our itinerary, we would in a sense be working backwards, so we will at this juncture concentrate on some key points in the location of this square mount and look at them in greater detail when we encounter each point later on in our tour.

LOCATING THE ORIGINAL 500-CUBIT-SQUARE TEMPLE MOUNT

The *Step*

The starting point of the research was the odd angle of the *step* at the northwest corner of the raised Muslim platform. The steps near the *Qubbat al-Khadr* are the only ones not built parallel to the walls of the platform, their direction being derived from the angle of the bottom *step*. This *step* is made up of a line of single ashlars, in contrast to the other steps of this flight, which are made up of many smaller stones. It appears therefore that this *step*, which is virtually parallel to the Eastern Wall of the Temple Mount, is, in effect, the remnant of an early wall. The central part of the Eastern Wall near the Golden Gate also contains masonry that is generally accepted as being of pre-Herodian origin, with a similar section further to the south. As the style of masonry used in the *step/ wall* resembles that found in the central section of the Eastern Wall, we have therefore

Plan of the Temple Mount showing its stages of development, with indications of the pre-Herodian 500-cubit-square Temple Mount.

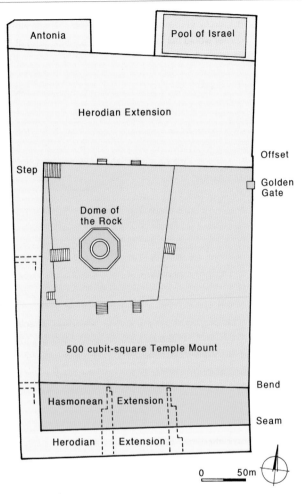

View of the northernmost large stone in "the step" that is precisely in line with the northern edge of the Raised Platform.

identified it as the Western Wall of the pre-Herodian Temple Mount.

Northern Rockscarp

Turning to the east, we see in the records of Warren that he found in Cistern 29, along the northern wall of the Raised Platform, the remains of a quarried rockscarp. Further remains of this scarp can be seen near the northeast corner of this platform, giving a distinct impression of having been sheared off to provide the foundation for a fortified wall. Projecting the line of the northern rockscarp westwards to the *step* and eastwards to the Eastern Wall, we find the distance to be 861 feet (262.50 m) long, exactly 500 cubits according to the Royal Cubit of 20.67 inches (0.525 m). This makes its identification with the Northern Wall of the square platform most likely. The northernmost stone of the *step* actually fits exactly in the right-angled corner with this Northern Wall. The projected northwest corner would fall just north of the Golden Gate, at 1,101 feet (335.60 m) north of the Herodian southeast corner. Some 38 feet (11.60 m) to the north of this northeast corner of the square Temple Mount, an *offset* can be seen, which probably was part of a projecting tower that may have been added here with defense in mind.

The Southern End of the Eastern Wall

A slight *bend* in the Eastern Wall helped locate the original southeast corner of the Temple Mount. On measurement, it was found to be situated exactly 500 cubits from the point where the proposed Northern Wall intersected the Eastern Wall. The intersection of perpendicular lines drawn west from the *bend* and south from the *step* give the location of the southwest corner. A thrilling confirmation of the location of the southwest corner of the square of 500 cubits was found in the L-shape of the Herodian underground stairway of Barclay's Gate. This particular shape was apparently meant to make construction easier. Herod's builders constructed the southern part of this stairway against the existing Western Wall instead of piercing through it. It would appear that the underground passageway of Warren's Gate was similarly built against the pre-Herodian Western Wall. Further confirmation was found in the underground passageways of the Double and Triple Gates. They are approximately 240 feet (73.20 m) long and terminate at the line of the proposed early Southern Wall, thus reflecting in their length the size of the southern extension of the square Temple Mount. With these points in mind, we can better orientate ourselves for the rest of the tour.

12. The Southeast Corner

The Eastern Wall of the Temple Mount is the most interesting of all as it is the only one that has masonry which predates the Herodian period. At the southeast corner Herodian masonry has been preserved to a great height. Thirty-five stone courses are still standing above bedrock, although only some twenty-one can be seen above ground. The Master Course continues around the corner for approximately 25 feet (8 m), after which it changes into regular Herodian masonry. At 66 feet (20 m) from the corner, a vertical line projects upwards from the eighth visible course above ground level. This is part of a tower that had three windows that can be seen higher up, to give the corner the impression of strength.

To the right of this tower, a small double entrance is visible above an arch and impost course. A stairway built over arches gave access from the street below, similar to Robinson's Arch, but on a smaller scale.

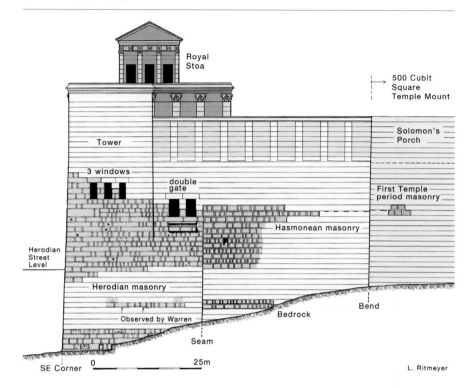

Reconstruction drawing of the southeast corner of the Temple Mount.

The "seam" near the southern end of the Eastern Wall. To the left of the seam is Herodian masonry, and to the right, Hasmonean.

Next to the double entrance, 106 feet (32 m) from the southeast corner, is a vertical joint (also known as the *seam*) in the wall. The masonry to the right (north) belongs to a Hasmonean extension to the original square Temple Mount. In 186 BCE Antiochus IV Epiphanes built the *Akra*, a fortress that housed a Macedonian garrison, to the south of the Temple Mount. In 141 BCE Simon the Maccabee destroyed the *Akra* and the space it occupied was added to the Temple Mount, together with adjacent areas.

View of the bend *in the Eastern Wall and Muhammad's Pillar.*

As we walk further to the north and look up, we see a column known as Muhammad's Pillar projecting from the wall. This feature dates from the Muslim period and has nothing to do with the Temple, but is a convenient marker for a very revealing element in the Eastern Wall. Warren noted that at this point 240 feet (73.20 m) from the southeast corner, the wall changes direction slightly. As this *bend* is located exactly 861 feet (262.5 m) or 500 cubits south of the projected northeast corner of the square Temple Mount, it provides archaeological evidence for the existence of the southeast corner of the square platform, which is probably preserved deep below ground. The *bend* can be seen with the naked eye when standing at the southeast corner, looking along the wall.

Types of ancient masonry found in the Eastern Wall.

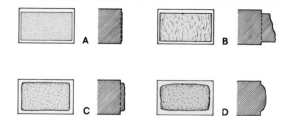

A. Herodian masonry with flat, smooth boss
B. Herodian masonry with unfinished boss
C. Hasmonean masonry with projecting boss
D. Iron Age masonry with bulging boss

Ancient Masonry in the Eastern Wall

Approximately 13 feet (4 m) north of the projected southeast corner, some massive ashlars can be seen at ground level. These, in contrast to the smooth bosses of Herodian stones and the rough projecting bosses of Hasmonean masonry, have rounded bulging bosses. This is a feature of masonry from the First Temple period and, as we shall see later, these five stones can be identified as belonging to the wall of the earlier square Temple Mount.

As we walk along the path, further massive stones can be seen near the present ground level on either side of the Golden Gate. The ashlars in the well-preserved 51-foot- (15.5-m-) long southern section and in the 68-foot- (20.7-m-) long northern section also have margins and roughly cut

Masonry from the time of the Kings of Judah (First Temple period) in the Eastern Wall..

Ashlars south of the Golden Gate which are typical of the First Temple period.

bosses, typical of the time of the Kings of Judah. The northern termination of this early masonry protrudes a couple of feet from the line of the Eastern Wall and we have called this point the *offset*.

13. The Golden Gate

The Golden Gate, around which swirl various traditions, is the most intriguing of all the gates of the Temple Mount. In Jewish tradition, it is through this gate (*Sha'ar haRachamim*—Gate of Mercy), blocked since the ninth century, that the Messiah will enter at the end of days, led in by the prophet Elijah. This is based on the prophecy of Ezekiel 44.1–3. Christians believe that Christ made his triumphal entry into Jerusalem (recorded in all four of the gospels) through this gate on the Sunday before his crucifixion (Palm Sunday). By riding on a donkey, he fulfilled the messianic prophecy recorded in Zechariah 9.9. Muslims refer to it as the Gate of Eternity (*Bab al-Dahariyeh*) and believe it will play an important part in the last judgment of mankind. The Muslim cemetery along the Eastern Wall is thought to have been placed there in the belief that the forerunner of Messiah, Elijah, being of a priestly family, could not pass through the Golden Gate, thus preventing the coming of the Messiah.

The Golden Gate's outer façade is composed of two blocked-up gateways adorned with intricately carved relief

Outer façade of the Golden Gate.

arches. The gate appears to have been built in the Umayyad period, on the foundations of an earlier gate. The remains of two massive ancient gateposts are preserved inside this gate. The gateposts are set in the same line as the Eastern Wall of the Temple Mount and line up with the massive masonry that can be seen on either side of the Golden Gate and farther south in the Eastern Wall. The gateposts and the three masonry sections appear therefore to be part of the same construction. The top of the southern gatepost is level with the top of the ancient masonry that can be seen south of the Golden Gate. The northern gatepost is one stone course higher and is located only one stone course below the surface of the Temple Mount. This means that the top of the original lintel would have been at the same height as the present-day ground-level of the Temple platform. This is

A cutaway reconstruction drawing of the Golden Gate.

The Golden Gate

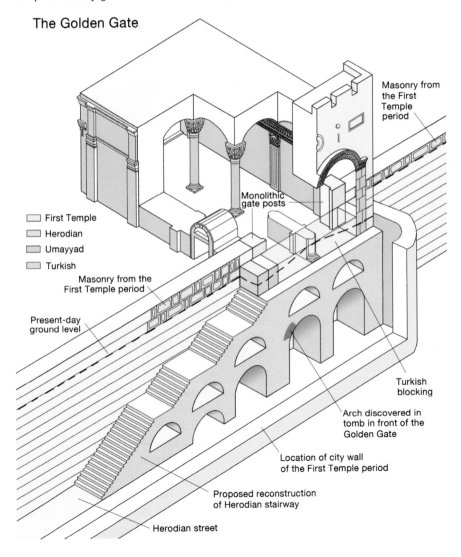

Masonry from the First Temple period

First Temple
Herodian
Umayyad
Turkish

Monolithic gate posts

Masonry from the First Temple period

Present-day ground level

Turkish blocking

Arch discovered in tomb in front of the Golden Gate

Location of city wall of the First Temple period

Proposed reconstruction of Herodian stairway

Herodian street

Arch found in tomb in front of the Golden Gate. (Photo: Obe Hokansen)

the same level as that of the *step*, the remains of the Western Wall of the square Temple Mount, located at the foot of the northwest stairway that leads up to the Raised Platform of the Dome of the Rock. The two gateposts belong to a gate that dates from the First Temple period and is most likely the Shushan Gate, mentioned in Mishnah *Middot* 1.3 as the only gate in the Eastern Wall. The gate most probably was given this name by builders who had returned from exile in Babylon and in whose memories the Palace of Shushan lived on.

It seems reasonable to suggest that the central section of the Eastern Wall dates from the First Temple period, in particular to the time of King Hezekiah. This square mount was extended south in the Hasmonean period, while both the southern and northern additions were made by King Herod the Great.

In 1969, the remains of an underground arch were discovered inside a grave in front of the Golden Gate. It was suggested that this may have been a pre-Herodian gateway. However, as the arch stones appear to be Herodian, it is more reasonable to suggest that this arch was part of a Herodian staircase leading up to the original gate. It is fascinating to contemplate that the stairway may still be intact under this gate, although hidden from sight by the Muslim Cemetery. We do know that the remains of an ancient city wall lie under the present-day path, where you are standing, as was discovered by Warren in the 1860s. The above-mentioned arched stairway led down through a gate in this city wall, the so-called *Miphkad* (Muster, or Inspection) Gate mentioned in Nehemiah 3.31, apparently still in use in the Second Temple period. During the latter period, it was through these gates that the Red Heifer was led out from the Temple Mount to the Mount of Olives (Mishnah, *Parah* 3.6). On the Day of Atonement, the Scapegoat was led by the same route into the wilderness (Mishnah, *Yoma* 6.4).

One would have expected to find the northeast corner of the square Temple Mount at a distance of 500 cubits from its southeast corner. This corner would have been located 39 feet (11.90 m) north of the Golden Gate. However, no vertical joint or other indications were found here in the wall. The ancient masonry actually continues for another 29 feet (8.84 m) as far as the *offset*. We have concluded therefore that this stretch must have belonged to an integral tower, built in order to protect the Temple Mount from the north. A tower in this location is actually mentioned in Nehemiah 3.31.

North of this *offset*, Herodian stones are encountered again up to the northeast corner of the present-day Temple Mount, although only one stone course is visible above ground. There are many more courses preserved

Remains of the Corner Tower mentioned in Nehemiah 3.31 are visible along this stretch of the city wall just north of the Golden Gate.

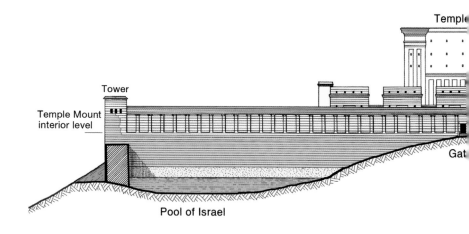

Tower

Temple Mount interior level

Temple

Gat

Pool of Israel

underground because at this section the Temple Mount wall crosses the deep Bezetha Valley. At the deepest point, a total of 48 Herodian stone courses have been preserved underground.

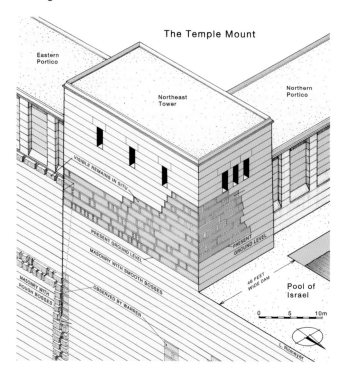

Reconstruction drawing of the Northeast Corner Tower.

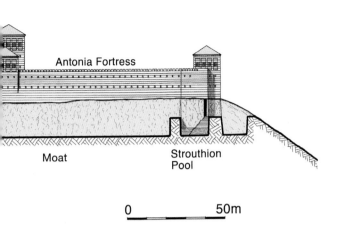

Reconstruction drawing of the Northern Wall of the Temple Mount.

Antonia Fortress

Moat

Strouthion Pool

0   50m

14. Northeast Corner Tower (east face)

At the northeast corner of the Temple Mount, eleven stone courses form the visible remains of a slightly projecting Herodian tower, while another 29 courses have been preserved underground. The other (northern) side of the corner can be seen on the inside of the city wall.

THE NORTHERN WALL—DISCOVERING THE HIDDEN WALL

Very little can be seen of the Northern Wall of the Temple Mount. Indeed, it is so difficult to discern and the overall effect is such a patchwork, that some have disputed that it can be identified as the northern façade wall of the Temple Mount. However, by careful observation, the persistent visitor can follow its course as far as the northwest corner.

Useful Information

There should be no problems with security when following the line of the Northern Wall, but the area is a bit run down. Although you will be walking along the well-trodden *Via Dolorosa* for part of the way, you will be required to dip in and out of buildings to trace the remains of this elusive wall. However, of all sections of the Temple Mount tour, this is the one that is best equipped for refreshments, so you can reward yourself for completing a full circuit of the Temple Mount walls with a cold drink from one of the enthusiastic young vendors along the way.

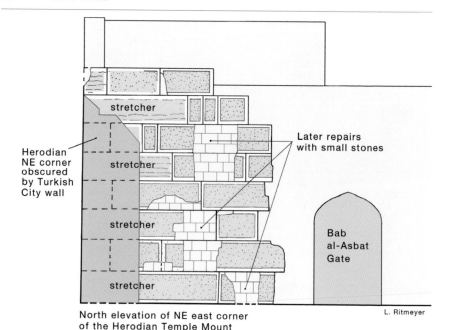

Herodian NE corner obscured by Turkish City wall

stretcher

stretcher

stretcher

stretcher

stretcher

Later repairs with small stones

Bab al-Asbat Gate

North elevation of NE east corner of the Herodian Temple Mount

L. Ritmeyer

Elevation of the north face of the Northeast Corner Tower.

Northeast Corner Tower (north face)

Walking from the cemetery to Lions' (St. Stephen's) Gate and turning left after going through the gate and continuing along the inside of the city wall, one reaches the *Bab al-Asbat* Gate, which is the easternmost of the northern gates to the present-day Temple Mount. The masonry between this gate and the city wall is crucial in proving that this is the line of the Northern Wall of the Temple Mount. Although the Herodian northeast corner is obscured by the Turkish city wall, stones from the Second Temple period of the typical header-and-stretcher construction are plainly visible and clearly belong to the northeast tower of the Herodian Temple Mount. The many small stones in between the larger ones are only surface repairs to the large Herodian stones of this tower.

15. Pool of Israel

The adjacent open-air visitor's center (al-Ghazali Square), with its block-shaped benches, lies over a large and deep water reservoir. This is the Herodian Pool of Israel that used to collect water from St. Anne's Valley, where the Bethesda

(above) View of the south wall of the Pool of Israel. The rough stones can be seen below the two windows.

(left) Model of the Pool of Israel, viewed from the east. (Photo: Philip Evans)

Pools are located, and may have been used as a reservoir for the Temple Mount. It also served as a moat to protect the Northern Wall.

Some of the internal stones of the southern wall of the Pool of Israel can be seen at the foot of the present-day Northern Wall of the Temple Mount.

16. Antonia Fortress

Return to the Lions' Gate Road (*Derech Sha'ar HaArayot/ al-Mujahideen* Road). Walking along this street, a ramp on the left side (at the First Station of the Cross, opposite the Church of the Flagellation) leads to the Umariyya School that is built on the platform of the Antonia Fortress that will be described below. Occasionally it is possible to enter the courtyard and get a glimpse of the Temple Mount through one of its windows. A bit further from the ramp along the *Via Dolorosa*, on the left can be seen a small section of the rockscarp which carried the northern wall of the Antonia Fortress.

Model of the Antonia Fortress, viewed from the northeast. (Photo: Philip Evans)

17. Strouthion Pool

Across the road, inside the Convent of the Sisters of Zion, one can visit the underground reservoir, known as the Strouthion Pool, which supplied the Antonia Fortress with water. Here the northern part of the pool is visible, while the southern part can be viewed at the end of the Western Wall Tunnel. The two parts are separated by a wall.

The view of the Temple Mount seen through one of the windows of the Umariyya School. (Photo: Alexander Schick)

Having reached the northwest corner of the Temple Mount, we have now completed our tour of its outer walls. This has hopefully oriented us to the size and significance of the site, its location between the Tyropoeon and Kedron Valleys and its ways of access. With this sense of place, we may take a well-earned break before proceeding to the next and final section of our tour.

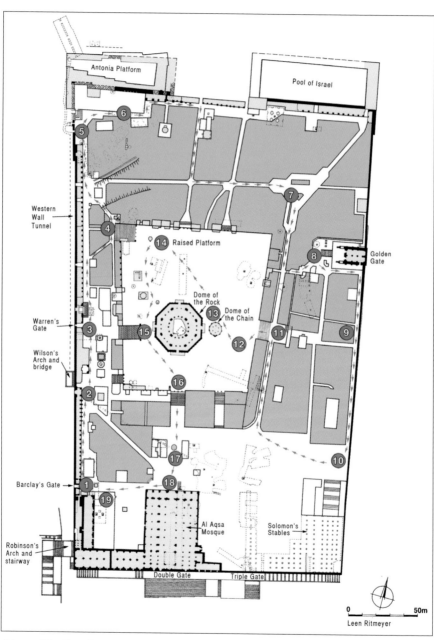

Antonia Platform

Pool of Israel

Western
Wall
Tunnel

Raised Platform

Golden
Gate

Warren's
Gate

Dome of
the Rock

Dome of
the Chain

Wilson's
Arch and
bridge

Barclay's Gate

Al Aqsa
Mosque

Solomon's
Stables

Robinson's
Arch and
stairway

Double Gate

Triple Gate

0   50m

Leen Ritmeyer

A tour of the Temple
Mount platform.

CHAPTER 3

A TOUR OF THE TEMPLE MOUNT PLATFORM

GOING UP TO THE MOUNTAIN OF THE HOUSE OF THE LORD

Encircling the walls of the Temple Mount will have given you some appreciation of its vast proportions and a sense of how it developed over time. However, it is but a preparation for the matchless experience of actually ascending to the platform and walking in the place that is at the center of God's purpose for man.

USEFUL INFORMATION

Admission to the Temple Mount is free. Entrance for non-Muslims is only through the Mughrabi Gate. You can exit through the same gate or through the Gate of the Chain. Security check for the Temple Mount is on the ramp leading up to the Mughrabi Gate. This is on the right-hand side of the Western Wall security entrance leading into the Plaza from the Dung Gate.

Opening hours can change depending on the political climate and on Muslim prayer times, but generally are as follows:

Summer—Sunday to Thursday: 7.30–11.30 a.m.; 1.30–2.30 p.m.

Winter—Sunday to Thursday: 7.30–10.30 a.m.; 12.30–1.30 p.m.

The queue can sometimes be long, so get in line early if you want to have enough time to do the site justice! The Mount is closed to tourists on Fridays and Saturdays and during the entire month of Ramadan. Non-Muslims are not permitted to enter the Dome of the Rock, the al-Aqsa Mosque, or indeed any of the other Muslim buildings on the site.

Modest dress is required—no shorts or bare shoulders. The extremely sensitive nature of the site means that no Bibles or prayer books, other than the Quran, are permitted on the Temple Mount, nor are weapons or religious Jewish items such as a *shofar* or prayer shawls. These could be left at the facility in the security area and retrieved after the visit. It is also forbidden to pray or to make gestures that look like praying. ID may be requested.

The site is sometimes closed without warning, thus it is advisable to call the Old City police station in advance to confirm that a visit is possible. Tel: 02-6226250.

This tour is not your average tour of the Temple Mount, which usually consists of a general explanation, a look at the exterior of the Dome of the Rock, a view of the Mount of Olives, a look at the exterior of the al-Aqsa Mosque and then out again. Apart from wanting to find out all there is to know about the site, an added benefit of exploring the Temple Mount off the beaten track is that it is generally quieter, offering more opportunities for thought and reflection.

MUGHRABI GATE ENTRANCE

This gate dates to about the twelfth century, at which stage the ground level above Barclay's Gate outside the Temple Mount had risen by several meters. Muslims from North Africa (the Maghreb), who arrived after Saladin's conquest of Jerusalem, settled in a neighborhood adjacent to the Western Wall, hence the name of the gate, *Bab al-Maghariba* (*Mughrabi*). In the aftermath of the 1967 Six-Day War, the keys to this gate were given to the Israeli army and it remains the only entrance to the Mount controlled by Israel.

The Mughrabi *Gate entrance to the Temple Mount.*

In 2004, a landslide caused the earthen ramp leading up to the gate to collapse. A wooden bridge was erected as

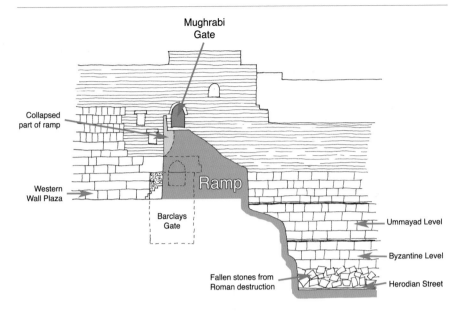

A sectional drawing showing the location of the Mughrabi *Gate* and ramp in relation to the Western Wall and the Temple Mount Excavations.

a temporary solution until a new and safer bridge could be built. Plans to replace this bridge with a more permanent structure have been dogged by controversy due to the sensitive nature of the location. You may take advantage of the view from the ramp to look down into the Southern Wall Excavations while waiting to enter the Temple Mount.

General Overview of the Platform

One's first impression on entering the Temple compound is that it is an oasis of calm in the midst of the congested Old City. A vast and dazzling paved area (the size of 24 football fields), with the looming golden Dome of the Rock at its heart, greets the eye. Clumps of trees provide welcome shade and here and there water tinkles from fountains (*sabils*) used for ritual washing by Muslims. Apart from the shrine of the Dome of the Rock on the Raised Platform, the *Haram al-Sharif* (Noble Sanctuary) contains an enormous lead-domed mosque called al-Aqsa, at the southern end of the platform. There are numerous other Muslim monuments that dot the area. These include secondary domes used for private prayer, prayer platforms (*musallas*) and niches (*mihrabs*). At present, there are eleven gates open in the

View of the platform with the Dome of the Rock in background—an "oasis of calm."

walls of the Temple Mount, but non-Muslims can only exit via the *Mughrabi* Gate or the Gate of the Chain (*Bab al-Silsila*) in the Western Wall.

Unsure of the location of the Holy of Holies, most rabbis declared the Temple Mount off-limits to religious Jews. However others, believing the Temple had stood on the site of the present-day Dome of the Rock and that the original holy area was restricted to the original 500-cubit square, allow Jews to visit and pray in all areas of the Temple Mount apart from the Raised Platform. It is becoming more and more acceptable for religious Jews to enter the compound, with parties of school children now among the visitors.

Muslims today deny any Jewish connection to the Mount and claim that the Israelis are trying to destroy the *Haram al-Sharif*. In recent years, the Waqf had gardens planted and pavements laid in order to conceal any early remains.

Given this zealous possessiveness, you may be surprised to see young Muslim boys blithely playing football between the monuments, a rather common sight. During school terms, children in school uniforms are also in evidence, as the Waqf runs three religious schools on the Temple Mount, an elementary school and separate high schools for boys and girls.

1. BARCLAY'S GATE INTERIOR

On entering the Temple Mount through the *Mughrabi* Gate you will see a small building on your left. Going round the corner, you can look through a window and see a room and a staircase. This staircase leads down to an underground chamber called the Mosque of al-Burak. On its southern wall an iron ring marks the place where Muhammad is believed to have tethered his legendary steed called Burak ("lightning"). From inside this underground chamber, the interior face of the lintel of Barclay's Gate can be seen. Although the gate that bears his name and is visible from the Western Wall Plaza is better known, it was from inside the Temple Mount that Barclay actually discovered this gate in 1854.

In the Herodian period, this chamber, together with two underground cisterns (Nos. 19 and 20; see plan of cisterns below, Appendix 2), formed the space in which an L-shaped stairway was constructed that led up from this gate to the Temple Mount. A small square domed building inside the *Mughrabi* Gate indicates the spot where the underground stairway used to turn southward. It would have surfaced onto the platform in front of the Islamic Museum. There a wellhead is located above Cistern 20.

Interior face of the lintel of Barclay's Gate

Interior view of the lintel of Barclay's Gate. (Photo: Matson collection)

2. MAMLUK PORTICO

Walking in a northerly direction along the inside of the Western Wall of the Temple Mount, we pass by a portico that dates from the Mamluk period (1250–1517). The Mamluks overthrew the Ayyubid dynasty of Egypt and founded a line of independent sultans who ruled in a period that was characterized by conflict and power struggle. Nevertheless, they undertook the greatest renovation of the city since the time of Herod the Great, with many buildings of a religious nature being erected on the Temple Mount. The Mamluk Portico is comprised of a series of vaults built against the Western Wall and open to the Temple Mount. Al-Nasir Muhammad Ibn Qalawun, Sultan of Egypt, constructed this portico in stages during the first half of the fourteenth century.

The Mamluk Portico clearly reflects the original porticoes of the Herodian Temple Mount, the difference being that the latter were double porticoes with flat roofs supported by beams laid on two rows of columns and anchored in the outer walls. Even today these porticoes offer shelter from

The southern end of the Mamluk Portico (above) and its northern end (right).

the hot summer sun and the cold winter rains.

Musallas

Walking along the west portico, one sees a low stone platform (*musalla* in Arabic). There are several of these platforms on the Temple Mount and they are designed to provide additional space for prayer. Most of them have a freestanding or built-in *mihrab*, a semicircular prayer niche oriented south, towards Mecca.

Qubbat Musa

The first small building to your right is *Qubbat Musa* (the Dome of Moses). It was built in 1249–50 during the last years of Ayyubid rule in Jerusalem on the west esplanade, close to *Bab al-Silsila*, the Gate of the Chain. It is a simple square building topped by an octagonal drum which carries a rounded stone dome. A semicircular *mihrab* can be seen at its south wall, between two rectangular windows.

Sabil Qasim Pasha

The octagonal Fountain of Qasim Pasha (*Sabil Qasim Pasha*) can be seen opposite the Gate of the Chain (*Bab

Qubbat Musa, *partly obscured by the tree on the right, with* Sabil Qasim Pasha *in the center and* Sabil Qaytbay *to its left. A musalla (low stone platform) can be seen at right, beneath the tree.*

Sabil Qasim Pasha.

al-Silsila). Next to it is a pool called the Fountain of the Bitter Orange (*Sabil al-Naranj*). This, the first Ottoman structure to be built in Jerusalem, in 1527 by Qasim Pasha, the Ottoman governor of the city, served as a fountain for drinking and ablutions. It has a finely stone-built dome and a lower canopy covered with lead sheets and supported by eight pillars. It was in use until the late 1940s.

Al-Madrasa al-Ashrafiyya

In 1482, when this theological college was built by order of Sultan al-Ashraf Qaytbay, it was considered to be the third most beautiful building on the Haram, after the Dome of the Rock and the al-Aqsa Mosque. Many of the typical Mamluk elements you see in its façade can be seen in a better state of preservation in the Cotton Merchants Gate just a bit further to the north along the west portico.

Sabil Qaytbay

This finest of all the Mamluk fountains in Jerusalem was built in 1482 by the sultan who also built the theological college just opposite. The *sabil* has a square base and is topped by a dome, beautifully decorated with stone arabesques. On its

The façade of al-Madrasa al-Ashrafiyya. (Photo: Dan Bahat)

south side is a Herodian sarcophagus that is decorated with rosettes. Used as a trough when the *sabil* was first built, it has now been filled in. However, on the left, the round side of the sarcophagus, where the head of the deceased was placed, can still be discerned as you face north.

The *sabil* is built over the underground passageway of Warren's Gate. In the Herodian period, the passageway would have turned south at this point and the stairway would have led up to the platform near the *mihrab* at the southern end of the *musalla* that is attached to the *Sabil Qaytbay*. Until recently, water used to be hauled up from Cistern no. 30 below (see plan of cisterns, Appendix 2).

The magnificent view of the Raised Platform and the Dome of the Rock, flanked by palm trees on the left and the *Qaytbay* on the right (cover photo and shown below) was

Sabil Qaytbay.

The Dome of the Rock, with a partial view of Sabil Qaytbay *to the right, as seen from the Ablution Gate (*Bab al-Matara).

taken from in front of the Ablution Gate (*Bab al-Matara*). A practical point worth noting here is that behind this gate are toilets that may be the oldest public toilets in the world still in use, hence the gate's name. They date to the Ayyubid period which followed the fall of Jerusalem to Saladin in 1187.

3. GATE OF THE COTTON MERCHANTS (*BAB AL-QATTANIN*)

The Gate of the Cotton Merchants stands at the eastern end of the Market of the Cotton Merchants that was built in 1336–37 by Tankiz en-Nasiri, governor of Syria, during the reign of Sultan al-Nasir Muhammad. This 312-foot- (95-m-) long market is a covered street with shops on both sides and flanked originally by two monumental gates. The Gate of the Cotton Merchants, built into the west portico, is one of the finest examples of Mamluk gate architecture and is a good place to familiarize yourself with the highly decorative style favored by this Muslim dynasty. In the gate's semi-

The beautifully decorated Gate of the Cotton Merchants.

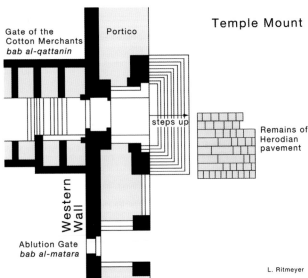

Plan of the Gate of the Cotton Merchants and remains of the Herodian pavement.

Gate of the Cotton Merchants
bab al-qattanin

Portico

Temple Mount

steps up

Remains of Herodian pavement

Western Wall

Ablution Gate
bab al-matara

L. Ritmeyer

vault, we see a superb example of stalactite corbeling (*muqarnas*). And above the doorway is an exquisite panel of interlocking contrasting red and cream stones. This *ablaq* technique of laying alternating courses of light and dark stone was adopted by the Mamluks in the fourteenth and fifteenth

Massive Herodian paving stones in front of the Gate of the Cotton Merchants.

centuries. You will have seen these elements before in the *Madrasa al-Ashrafiyya*, but here they are in an excellent state of preservation.

In front of the Gate of the Cotton Merchants, at a distance of 45 feet (13.70 m) from the Western Wall, there is a stretch of ancient paving stones. These massive stones appear to be Herodian in origin and are laid in an east-west direction. As the width of the double porticoes that Herod the Great constructed around the Temple Mount was about 45 feet (15 m) including the thickness of the Western Wall, we see before us a remnant of the pavement that was laid next to the west portico. This is one of the few places on the Temple Mount where one can walk on paving stones that have survived the Roman destruction of 70 CE and subsequent depredations of the site.

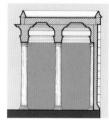

A sectional drawing of the Herodian west portico.

4. THE *STEP*

Moving along in a northerly direction brings you to one of the most interesting and evocative remains of the ancient Temple Mount. Stop at the northwest corner of the raised Muslim platform. Here we are standing at one of the eight flights of steps, topped by arcades that lead up to the platform of the Dome of the Rock. These steps are the only ones not built parallel to the walls of the platform, their direction being derived from the angle of the bottom step. This *step* is made

Close-up view of the step, at the bottom of the stairway leading to the Raised Platform.

up of a line of single ashlars, in contrast to the others of this flight that are comprised of many smaller stones. It appears therefore that this *step*, which is parallel to the Eastern Wall of the Temple Mount, is, in effect, the remains of an early wall. The rock contour maps from the nineteenth century indicate that this line of stones is built directly on the bedrock and is therefore the only single stone course in this area that survived the Roman destruction in 70 CE.

The Eastern Wall, in sections near the *bend* and near the Golden Gate, as we have seen above, also contains masonry that pre-dates the Herodian period. As the style of masonry used in this *step*/wall resembles that found in the

This photograph, taken in 2012, shows the step *with indications of the northwest corner of the pre-Herodian Temple Mount.*

sections of the Eastern Wall, we have therefore identified it as the western wall of the pre-Herodian Temple Mount. This research has led to the establishment of the location of the 500-cubit-square Temple Mount, which is believed to have been built in the time of Hezekiah.

Jesus' Prophecy

This is a good spot to think about the meaning of the words of Jesus as related in Matthew 24.2: "There shall not be left here one stone upon another that shall not be thrown down." He said this in response to the disciples who wanted to show him the buildings of the Temple. What we see here is the only surviving stone course of one of the walls that surrounded the inner courts of Herod's Temple Mount.

The original adjoining pavement near the bottom step has been overlaid with new pavers that are higher and conceal the protruding boss of the southernmost ashlar in the bottom step. However, a photograph, taken in 1972, confirms its original appearance. The northernmost large stone in the *step* is precisely in line with the northern edge of the Raised Platform.

This 1972 photograph shows the protruding boss of the southernmost ashlar in the step, *which has since been overlaid with new paving stones.*

Arcades

This is a good place to admire one of the graceful arcades (*qanatir*) located above the eight stairways that connect the courtyard and the Raised Platform. These consist of several pillars supporting three to five arches. Muslim tradition has it that scales (*mawazin*) will be suspended from these arcades on the Day of Judgment, to weigh the souls of those being judged. All of these arcades date from either the Ayyubid or Mamluk period.

Qubbat al-Khadr

On the right of the flight of steps that leads to the Raised Platform at its northwest corner, stands a small and delicate structure. This is the *Qubbat al-Khadr* or Dome of St. George. Six slender marble columns support six arches that bear a small pointed dome. Muslims pray to al-Khadr, identified by Christians as St. George, who is reputed to have slain a dragon. According to Muslim tradition, al-Khadr used to live in Jerusalem and often prayed on the Temple Mount.

Qubbat al-Khadr.

Fosse

In recent years, the area north of the Raised Platform has been planted with many olive trees. The large quantity of soil brought here obscures some important features of the Temple Mount. Warren describes an "excavated ditch", which he found 52 feet (15.85 m) north of the stairway at the northwest corner of the Raised Platform. Strabo, the Greek geographer and historian, describes this moat or "fosse" and gives its measurements as 60 feet (18.30 m) deep and 250 feet (76.20 m) wide. From a defensive point of view, the importance of the fosse is obvious, as it completes the natural

boundary to the north of the pre-Herodian Temple Mount, linking the Tyropoeon or Central Valley on the west with the Bezetha Valley that runs eastward into the Kedron Valley. The approach to the Temple Mount from the north was thus effectively cut off.

The same fosse, together with the Bezetha Valley, is recorded by Josephus (*Ant.* 14.60–62) as having been filled in by Pompey's soldiers in 63 BCE, thereby enabling them to storm the defensive towers at the northwest corner of the square Temple Mount. These towers, which belonged to the Hasmonean *Baris* Fortress, stood here in that space of 52 feet (15.85 m) between the stairway leading up to the Raised Platform and the fosse. In First Temple times, the towers of Hananeel and Meah stood here in this same space. Mentioned in Jeremiah 31.28 for the first time, they would have protected Hezekiah's square Temple Mount at the northwest corner.

Herodian paving stones between the fosse and the Antonia in the northern part of the Temple Mount. This photograph was taken in 1973, before the area was covered with a thick layer of soil and planted with olive trees.

Herodian Paving

North of this fosse and now buried beneath olive trees are the remains of a section of pavement that dates to the Herodian period. It is featured in many nineteenth-century photographs taken from the Antonia platform where the Turkish barracks were located. Two of the largest pavers measure 7 by 8.5 feet (2.14 by 2.59 m). Although no longer visible, just being aware of these stones deep under our feet helps us visualize the beautifully paved Herodian Temple courts.

5. THE "WINDOW" OF JOHN OF GISCHALA

Inside view of the "window" of John of Gischala. Through the hole in the ground at bottom left, Charles Warren reached this room from inside the Rock-hewn Aqueduct. The small window that was made between the two pilasters is therefore the only place through which the Rock-hewn Aqueduct can be reached from the Temple Mount platform.

Just before one reaches the northernmost gate in the Western Wall of the Temple Mount, the *Bab el-Ghawanima*, there is a small window on the left-hand side. This window was already noticed by Charles Warren in the 1860s. On the inside is a little room with two pilasters, most likely Herodian in origin. From here, in the Second Temple period, one could have entered the Rock-hewn Aqueduct, which can now be seen at the end of the Western Wall Tunnel.

According to Josephus, the Roman siege of the Antonia was protracted because the Jews, under the leadership of John of Gischala, had destroyed the Roman earthworks. John had used underground passageways to gain access to the area beneath the Antonia Fortress water reservoir (the Strouthion Pool), to undermine these earthworks and set them on fire (*War* 5.466–472). The Rock-hewn Aqueduct could only have been reached through this "window" that was probably made by John of Gischala to gain access.

The "window" of John of Gischala.

The western rockscarp that probably formed part of the base for the southwest tower of the Antonia Fortress built by King Herod.

6. ANTONIA FORTRESS

At the northwest corner of the Temple Mount, a rockscarp can be seen in the west wall north of the *Bab al-Ghawanima*. This western rocky wall that forms a corner with the rockscarp on which the Umariyya School is located, stands to a height of 32 feet (9.75 m). These vertical rockscarps once formed the base for the Antonia Fortress that Herod built here. They show the considerable portion of the mountain he must have cut away to create a platform for a fortress that, according to Josephus, was a "guard to the Temple." The Antonia Fortress had four towers, three of which were 50 cubits (86 ft./26.25 m) high and the fourth, the southeast tower, 70 cubits (120 ft./36.75 m) high. The view from this highest tower, that, according to Josephus "commanded a view of the whole area of the Temple" (*War* 5.242), must have been spectacular. The towers undoubtedly had openings for shooting arrows and larger windows for hurling heavy objects on assailants.

In the Herodian period, porticoes were also built along the inside of the Temple Mount walls. If you look carefully, five of the sockets of the north portico can still be seen in the rockscarp, in between the tall trees that have been planted in front. The horizontal beams that supported the roof rested in these sockets. The 19-inch (48-cm) square

The Antonia rockscarp in which sockets of the north portico can still be seen.

sockets are located at a height of 29 feet (8.80 m) above the rocky ground. Above these sockets several Herodian stone courses are visible.

Behind the Ghawanima minaret, the rock is set back a little from the line of the northern wall of the Temple Mount. In the Herodian period, a staircase led up to the roof where the north and west porticoes joined. From this place the fortress could be entered.

Paul and the Steps of the Antonia

Another New Testament scene can be visualized here. Looking up, we can imagine the staircase that led from the Temple Mount to the Antonia Fortress that was the backdrop to the scene portrayed in Acts 21 and 22. This was when Paul was falsely accused in the Temple of bringing a Gentile into the Sanctuary. A great commotion among the Jews ensued, with Paul being carried up the steps of the Antonia by a unit of Roman soldiers to save him from being killed. The Roman captain, Lysias, allowed Paul to address his fellow countrymen from the safety of the Antonia, probably from the top of the north portico, traces of which we can see here in front of us. Paul delivered his impassioned defense in the Hebrew tongue. In the courtyard of this fortress, he was bound with cords and prepared for scourging, which was only averted by his appealing to his Roman citizenship. Proposals that this was the Praetorium of the Gospels have been discounted and it is now the belief that the Praetorium was located in Herod's Palace in the west of the city.

Madrasa al-Isardiyya

Passing the Antonia rockscarp at the northern edge of the Haram, we see three notable buildings. The first is called *al-Isardiyya* and has the most beautifully crafted façade on the Haram, apparently from the fourteenth century as attested by early manuscripts. The building is divided into two parts by a Herodian wall, part of the original Antonia Fortress, and its construction shows much ingenuity, sitting as it does on the platform of the Antonia. One used to be able to see the Antonia rockscarp through these lower arches, but these

A cutaway reconstruction drawing of the Antonia Fortress.

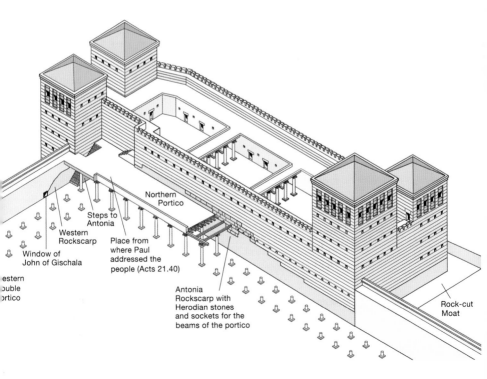

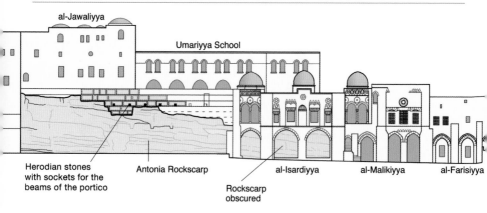

al-Jawaliyya

Umariyya School

Herodian stones
with sockets for the
beams of the portico

Antonia Rockscarp

Rockscarp
obscured

al-Isardiyya   al-Malikiyya   al-Farisiyya

*South elevation
of the Antonia
rockscarp. Some
of the sockets for
the beams of the
Herodian portico
can still be seen
in between the
trees. The three
lower arches of
al-Isardiyya have
been blocked off by
walls, obscuring the
view of the Antonia
rockscarp.*

have now been blocked by masonry.

The façade is in three parts and reflects the layout of the rooms behind it. A long assembly hall stands behind the intermediate buttresses and is supported by two cross-vaulted bays of the portico. Above these vaults, we see the most prominent feature in the façade, the semicircular *mihrab* of the assembly hall that juts out of the external wall. Although the building was originally a *madrasa* (a Muslim religious school) and then a library, today it is exclusively a residential building.

To the east of *al-Isardiyya* are two more buildings, *al-Malikiyya* and *al-Farisiyya*. All these buildings stand on the Antonia rockscarp that begins to rise westward under *al-Farisiyya*.

Qubbat Suleiman

Looking south from these buildings, down a paved path, we see the free-standing *Qubbat Suleiman*, built in the Crusader period as an open-air structure. Its arches are supported by eight pillars forming an octagon, above which is a drum that supports the dome. It was built in memory of King Solomon who built the First Temple.

In the Ayyubid period, the building was enclosed by walls, with a door placed in the north and a *mihrab* in the south. A small piece of rock, *Qubbat as-Sakhra as-Saira*, protrudes above the floor. It is possibly a high piece of bedrock around which the structure was built. According to legend, it was a fragment of the Foundation Stone.

Qubbat Suleiman.

Following the path that leads south towards the Raised Platform, we pass by the *Sabil al-Sultan Suleiman*, a fountain donated in the Ottoman period by Suleiman the Magnificent. Beside that is the Pavilion of Mahmoud II (1817–19). This is a small domed structure resting on four piers, also known as the Dome of the Lovers of the Prophets.

7. THRONE OF SOLOMON (*KURSI SULEIMAN*)

Continue on the path towards the Raised Platform, but turn left at the first opportunity. This brings you to a large junction. We are now getting closer to the Eastern Wall. This is a good spot to stop and take in another building that is linked to King Solomon. Commonly known as the Throne of Solomon or *Kursi Suleiman*, it is located just north of the Golden Gate and adjoins the Eastern Wall. It appears to have been built in the Ottoman period. Islamic tradition has it that here the king prayed after having completed the

Kursi Suleiman.

Ancient masonry at the northeast corner of the Raised Platform.

building of the temple. It is a closed, rectangular structure, roofed by a flat ceiling with two domes; the western section is used as a mosque.

From this junction, walk in a southerly direction, parallel to the Eastern Wall. On your right, just opposite the Golden Gate, you pass by the northeast corner of the Raised Platform. Here, three well-built stone courses are visible which predate the present-day Raised Platform and lie on the northern boundary of the original square Temple Mount.

Near this corner is a wellhead built over Cistern 28 (see plan of cisterns below, Appendix 2). A small cistern, it was built just against the original boundary line of the square Temple Mount, confirming the location of the latter.

8. THE GOLDEN GATE

In front of us is the interior façade of the Golden Gate, the exterior of which we observed while walking along the Eastern Wall. You may wish to refer back to the relevant notes for site information (see previous chapter). The decorative arches of its twin portals are identical to those in the eastern façade. These are approached by twenty-two descending steps, as the ground here falls off steeply into the Kedron Valley. On this side too the gates have been blocked, apart from two small openings, which allow access to the building. The door on the right is known as *Bab al-Rachmeh* (Door of Mercy), while that on the left is *Bab al-Tawbah* (Door of Repentance). Late in the gate's history two buttresses were added in order to stabilize the building.

In the twelfth century, the Muslim theologian and mystic Imam al-Ghazali (sometimes known as the Thomas Aquinas of Islam) is thought to have written his treatise "Revival of

The interior façade of the Golden Gate as viewed from the Temple Mount.

"The Scapegoat", a 19th-century painting by William Holman Hunt which depicts the scapegoat described in the Book of Leviticus.

the Religious Sciences" while living on the Temple Mount above these gates.

This usually deserted spot on the Temple Mount is a good place to stop and absorb much of Jerusalem's history and its longings. A convenient seating area is located beside a wellhead located over Cistern 15 (see plan of cisterns below, Appendix 2), which was quarried just inside the northern wall of the 500-cubit-square Temple Mount. There is so much to reflect on here, the expectations of all three monotheistic religions as regards the Last Days and the significance of this place in the route of the Scapegoat and Red Heifer. Another possible association is with the Beautiful Gate of the Temple mentioned in Acts 3.2,10. The earliest Greek New Testament uses the word 'oraia' for 'beautiful'. In the fourth century, Jerome's Latin Vulgate translation of the Bible used instead a word that sounded much like this word, the Latin word 'aurea', which means 'golden'. Thus the name "Golden Gate" was born. However, from the context of the miracle of Peter's healing of the lame man, it seems that this was performed near one of the other gates of the Temple Mount, with the Double Gate being the most likely candidate.

Cedar Beams near the Golden Gate

At the time of writing, large cedar beams were lying in the sunken area on the north side of the Golden Gate, out of view unless you look for them. These have a story to tell. After the damage to the al-Aqsa Mosque from the earthquakes of

1927 and 1937, the roof of the mosque was dismantled and the beams replaced with new ones. The old beams were left to the elements and moved from place to place. (They could well have been moved again by the time you read this.)

Despite their dilapidated state, some of the massive beams still carry decorations such as rosettes and foliage designs executed in typical Byzantine style, possibly remnants of the Nea Church that was uncovered in the Jewish Quarter Excavations. However, one of the beams has been carbon-dated to the first century BCE, still others to the ninth century BCE. Although we cannot say with any certainty, it is possible that these beams were originally used in the First and Second Temples, survived the Roman destruction, were reused in the Byzantine period and again incorporated into the al-Aqsa Mosque—mute witnesses to a turbulent history.

Cedar wood had to be transported from distant Lebanon (see reference to the use of the wood in Solomon's Temple in 1 Kings 5.6–10) and so would not have been easily discarded. There was another reason why it was worth "recycling." Like oak wood, cedar wood does not burn easily. When large beams are exposed to fire, only the outer layer

Cedar beams lying north of the Golden Gate. Carbon dating has shown that some of the beams date as far back as the time of the two temples.

View of the damaged ashlars remaining on the Temple Mount.

is charred while the core usually remains untouched. This extraordinary durability could explain why some of the Temple's roof beams may have survived while no stone of the Temple was left upon another after the Roman destruction of 70 CE.

As mentioned earlier, a large area on the Temple Mount near the southeast corner was illegally bulldozed in 2000 by the Waqf and most of the debris dumped in the Kedron Valley. At the time of writing, one can still see many damaged ashlars and remains of ancient columns lying in areas south of the Golden Gate. Some of these stones belonged to ancient buildings.

From there one can walk along to the Eastern Wall where Solomon's Porch used to be located.

9. SOLOMON'S PORCH

At present there are no porticoes along the Eastern and Southern Walls of the Temple Mount. In the Herodian period, however, there were porticoes on all sides. The eastern stoa pre-dated the others and was already colonnaded in the Hasmonean period. As we saw earlier, it stood directly over the wall of the earlier square Temple Mount and at the time of Herod the Great, was known as Solomon's Porch. This does not necessarily mean that it was built by this famous king, but certainly by one of Herod's predecessors. Offering welcome shelter from sun, wind and rain, it was obviously used as a place of congregation. Josephus provides us with a vivid description:

> The porticoes, all in double rows, were supported by columns five and twenty cubits high—each a single block of the purest white marble—and ceiled with panels of cedar. The natural magnificence of these columns, their excellent polish and fine adjustment presented a striking spectacle.   (*War* 5.190–192)

It was here that Jesus was almost stoned one wintry day during the feast of *Hanukkah* (John 10.22–39, where it is called the Feast of Dedication). This feast commemorated the cleansing of the Temple by Judah the Maccabee after Antiochus IV Epiphanes desecrated it in 167 BCE. Standing here on the inside of this Eastern Wall, we can imagine him

Present-day site of "Solomon's Porch".

speaking with his disciples, while around them in the Temple precincts, the people celebrated God's intervention in the restoration of their place of worship. Acts 3.11 and 5.12 also provide us with images of the time when the disciples used to congregate and teach here after the death of their master.

10. *AL-MARWANI*

Nearing the southeast corner of the Temple Mount one can see a massive newly built stairway descending from the platform level to an underground arched construction. This enormous structure was mistakenly called Solomon's Stables by the Crusaders. The arches at the bottom of the steps were closed up to recent times, but in 1996, two of these were opened to provide access to the underground vaulted area, converted into a mosque known as *al-Marwani*. Large-scale earthworks were carried out by the Waqf following this operation, particularly during the years 1999–2000. In 2004, in order to preserve as many ancient remains as possible, Israeli archaeologists, under the auspices of the Bar-Ilan University, established the Temple Mount Sifting Project. This sifts the debris moved to nearby Emek Tzurim National Park (located at the foot of Mount Scopus—not visible from this spot). Thousands of volunteers take part in this daily year-round project, with every bucket containing artifacts

In this large tent on the western slope of Mount Scopus, the debris that was illegally excavated and removed from the Temple Mount is being sifted. (Photo: Nick Barnes)

which reveal part of the history of the Temple Mount. Sadly, it is not possible to determine where exactly on the Temple Mount these finds originated, if at all. One of the most noteworthy discoveries was a *bulla* (clay sealing) bearing evidence of ancient Hebrew writing and administrative activity in First Temple times.

Solomon's Stables and the Cradle of Jesus

The large vaults inside this space now used as a Muslim prayer hall are apparently of Umayyad origin. When the al-Aqsa Mosque was built, the whole of the Southern Wall was repaired and these vaults were built to support the southeast corner. In the Crusader period, the arched structure was used to stable horses, hence the name Solomon's Stables.

After wet-spraying over a sieve, the debris is being examined and important finds reserved for research. (Photo: Nick Barnes)

Prior to the construction of the *al-Marwani* mosque, if one wanted to enter the stables (in the days when access was permitted to non-Muslims), one went through a small doorway at the southeast corner of the Temple Mount. Descending a short winding staircase, one entered a little room just below the surface of the Temple Mount. (Another staircase continues down to the level of the stables.) Inside this little room are three windows, one in the Southern Wall and two in the Eastern Wall. These appear to be Herodian in origin, as does the springer of a vault located above the eastern windows. This indicates that the southeast corner of the Temple Mount was also vaulted in the Herodian period and was probably used to store items connected with the Temple services and brought in through the Triple Gate.

The so-called Cradle of Jesus, located in a small room at the southeast corner of the Temple Mount.

There is a small domed shrine, the so-called Cradle of Jesus (*Sidna Issa*; see Plan of Muslim Buildings, Appendix 3), in this little room. The lower part of this shrine is a Byzantine altar with four pillars and a reliquary underneath. This may be connected with the fact that in the Early Christian period, a monastery was located just outside the Southern Wall of the Temple Mount, between the Triple Gate and the southeast corner. The altar was later capped by a small dome, possibly in the Early Muslim period. Islam also reveres Jesus as a prophet.

The eastern steps leading to the Raised Platform of the Temple Mount, with the Dome of the Rock in background.

11. THE COURT OF THE WOMEN

Turning around again to the north, we walk towards the steps that lead up to the raised Muslim platform from the east. This is a favorite place for taking photographs. Sitting on the steps, those being photographed have a magnificent view towards the Mount of Olives and the graceful archways create a beautiful frame for a picture. It is also a good place to identify and picture elements of the Herodian Temple Mount (see Appendix 1 below). Standing at the bottom of this flight of steps, you are at the center of where the Court of the Women used to be.

This court also housed the Treasury, mentioned in the story of the widow's mites. Here, under the colonnades that surrounded the court on three sides, were thirteen trumpet-shaped boxes into which the people dropped their monetary offerings. The widow would have dropped her two tiny coins into one of the boxes called Freewill Offerings. The tinkling sound made by the tiny coins would have given away the financial value of her offering, but Jesus recognized the true value of her contribution.

There were unroofed chambers in

A view of the Mount of Olives from the eastern steps. The pavement at the foot of the steps corresponds to the location of the Court of the Women (Treasury).

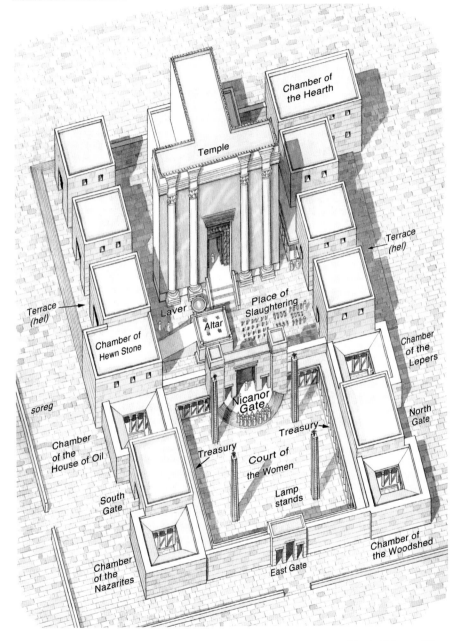

Chamber of
the Hearth

Temple

Terrace
(hel)

Terrace
(hel)

Place of
Slaughtering

Laver

Altar

Chamber of
Hewn Stone

Chamber
of the
Lepers

soreg

Nicanor
Gate

North
Gate

Chamber
of the
House of Oil

Treasury

Treasury

Court of
the Women

South
Gate

Lamp
stands

Chamber of
the Woodshed

Chamber
of the
Nazarites

East Gate

each of the four corners of the Court of the Women. The Chamber of the Nazarites, where the Nazarite cut off his hair in completion of his vow was in the southeast corner of

The buildings of the Herodian Temple compound.

Model of the Court of the Women in front of the Nicanor Gate to the Holy Temple. (Photo: Philip Evans)

this court (No. 9 in the Plan of New Testament links, Appendix 1 below). The Chamber of the House of Oil, used to store the oil and wine needed for the Temple service, was on the southwest. The Chamber of the Lepers, where the lepers bathed as part of their cleansing stood in the northwest (No. 8 in the Plan of New Testament links), while the Chamber of the Woodshed, which stored the wood used on the Altar, was in the northeast. The massive lampstands used in the Feast of the Water-drawing (*Bet haSho'eva*) during the Feast of Tabernacles would have towered above on either side of the staircase. The remaining two would have stood just to the east making a square formation.

Nicanor Gate

If you were to climb the eastern steps some two thousand years ago, you would have been standing atop the fifteen semi-circular steps that led up to the Nicanor Gate. The Levites used to stand on these steps and recite the 15 Songs of Ascents (Psalms 120–134). These steps have never been excavated, but must lie underneath the modern steps. It is quite overwhelming to think that the remains of the Nicanor Gate may still lie directly beneath the Muslim archway you see today. It would have been to this gate that Mary, the mother of Jesus, brought her sacrifice of two young pigeons for her purification after the birth of her son (Luke 2.22–24). Also in the Second Temple period, a cleansed leper would have come here after bathing in the Chamber of the Lepers. A priest would then perform the required ritual, after which the healed leper was allowed to enter the Temple court. Another purification ritual that took place here was for the woman suspected of adultery, described in Numbers 5.

Now, although your tour can help visualize the various buildings of the Temple, for females, this would have been as far as they were allowed to venture into the sacred precincts

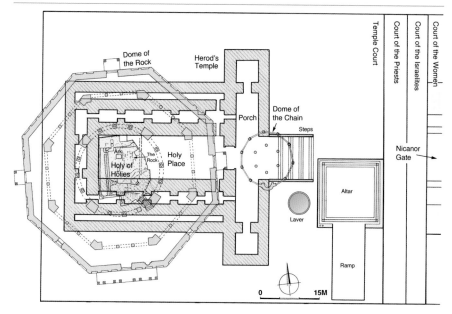

Dome of
the Rock

Herod's
Temple

Porch

Dome of
the Chain

Steps

Ark

The
Rock

Holy
Place

Holy of
Holies

Laver

Altar

Ramp

Nicanor
Gate

Temple Court

Court of the Priests

Court of the Israelites

Court of the Women

0   15M

in Temple times. As males, you could have continued into the narrow Court of the Israelites, on the other side of the Nicanor Gate. Entry to the Temple Court proper was restricted only to the priests. Even King Herod himself was prohibited from entering these inner courts, even though the rebuilding of Solomon's Temple was the greatest achievement of this Master-builder!

Floor plan of Herod's Temple and the large altar. The present-day Dome of the Rock and Dome of the Chain are shaded in blue for easy orientation.

12. ALTAR LOCATION

The huge Altar of Burnt Sacrifice, with its ramp ascending from the south, would have lain in the open space (no. 4 in the Plan of New Testament links, Appendix 1 below) between the modern-day steps and the Dome of the Chain.

A view of the Dome of the Rock with the Dome of the Chain to its east. The location of the Altar is indicated.

(And of course, if we wish to go further back in history, we can remind ourselves that here, too, is the place of Araunah's Threshing Floor.) Looking from the top of these steps, the Shambles or Place of Slaughtering would have been visible on the right. The Laver would have stood just southeast of the Dome of the Chain.

Altar location

Close-up view of the Dome of the Chain, with the Dome of the Rock in background, looking west.

13. DOME OF THE CHAIN (*QUBBAT AL-SILSILA*)

This enigmatic construction is located on the east of the Dome of the Rock and looks like a miniature version of the latter building. In fact, some early Arab historians suggest that it was used as a model for the famed shrine. It stands virtually in the center of the Temple Mount, on the original site of the Porch of Herod's Temple. A hexagonal construction, supported on columns, bears the small dome, while eleven pillars carry the outer polygonal arcade, which has a mihrab in the south. The building is open on all sides and the interior is covered with beautiful mosaics and colored stonework.

The Dome of the Chain is believed to have been built by Abd al-Malik in 691. It has also been suggested that it may have served as the treasury of the Haram. According to Islamic tradition, it is here that a chain will separate the wicked from the just on the final Day of Judgment.

14. DOME OF THE SPIRITS (*QUBBAT AL-ARWAH*)

Walking about 330 feet (100 m) to the northwest of the Dome of the Rock, we come to a small domed structure, known as the Dome of the Spirits. The fact that underneath this modest cupola lies what some have suggested to be bare bedrock has given rise to a theory that it marks the location of the Foundation Stone of the Holy of Holies of the Temple. Asher Kaufman, a Jerusalem physicist, published his conclusion in 2004; he believes that the Temple Mount was of an irregular shape, wide on the eastern side while narrowing towards the west. He understands the Temple's alignment to have been on a line through the Golden Gate to the top of the Mount of Olives, so that the Dome of the Rock could not have been built on the site of the Temple.

Dome of the Spirits.

The Herodian paving stone under the Dome of the Spirits and (below) plan.

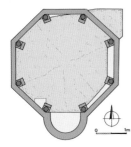

However, careful examination of the stone under the dome makes it clear that the evidence for this theory is flimsy. Firstly, the bedrock contour map made by the reliable Warren shows that the bedrock here is located at least 10 feet (3 m) below this stone. The Rock under the Dome of the Rock is about 15 feet (5 m) higher, so Kaufman's location contradicts the statement of Josephus that the Temple was constructed on top of the hill. Secondly, from comparisons made between this stone and large paving slabs found in front of the Double and Triple Gates, it is obvious that this too is a Herodian paving slab. The rectangular projection at the northeast corner would have allowed for a smaller paving stone to be placed next to it, a common feature in Herodian paving. From a topographical point of view, the fact that the northern court of Kaufman's Temple would fall into the Bezetha Valley also makes his theory untenable.

A comparison of the Herodian paving slabs found below the Dome of the Spirits and those in the Southern Wall of the Temple Mount.

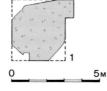

HERODIAN PAVING SLABS

1. Below Qubbat el-Arwah
2. In front of the Double Gate
3. In front of the Triple Gate

Dome of al-Khalili

Walking along the west side of the Dome of the Rock, we encounter a square domed building that was built over an ancient rockscarp, namely the Dome of al-Khalili (the Hebronite). This early eighteenth-century building, dedicated to Sheikh Muhammad al-Khalili, is also known as *Hujirat Bakhin Bakhin*. To its immediate northeast is a wellhead that belongs to Cistern 3 (see plan of Cisterns, Appendix 2, below). According to our plan of the

Dome of al-Khalili.

Temple and its courts (p. 29), the Chamber of the Hearth was located above this cistern which has several chambers, one or more of which apparently contained facilities for bathing. *Middot* 1.6 records that the room in the northwest had a staircase that descended to the *mikveh*. At the time of writing, the building was used as the office for the architect of the Temple Mount.

Dome of the Ascension.

Dome of the Ascension (*Qubbat al-Miraj*)

This octagonal building stands about 65 feet (20 m) northwest of the Dome of the Rock. Originally, the spaces between the pointed arches were open, but they were later blocked in. There are pairs of marble columns at the corners, capped by typical Crusader capitals. Above the dome is a small onion dome resting on six miniature columns.

It was constructed between 1140 and 1150, probably as a baptistery of the *Templum Domini* (Temple of the Lord), as the Crusaders called the Dome of the Rock when they used it as a church. However, in Muslim tradition this spot is held to be the place where Muhammad ascended into Heaven, and writers of the early Arab period describe a structure that predated the structure we see here today. The Crusader building in turn was renovated in 1200 by the Ayyubids.

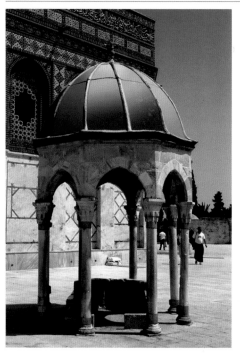

Dome of the Prophet.

Dome of the Prophet (*Qubbat al-Nabi*)

This small structure stands between the Dome of the Ascension and the Dome of the Rock. The lead-covered hemispherical dome rests on eight marble columns that support multi-colored pointed arches. It was built in 1539 to mark the site where Muhammad led the prophets in prayer before his ascension into Heaven.

15. THE DOME OF THE ROCK

Although at the time of publication, the Dome of the Rock and the al-Aqsa Mosque are closed to visitors, full information is provided here. The Dome of the Rock is one of those iconic buildings that is known to virtually everybody on the planet. The golden dome that shimmers against the cobalt blue sky and the blue tiled walls of the octagonal building are both contrasting and harmonious.

The Dome of the Rock is the crowning glory of early Islamic architecture. It was built by order of Abd al-Malik to commemorate Muhammad's Night Journey and was completed in 692. Its octagonal shape is reminiscent of Byzantine churches that are designed to commemorate a certain sacred event or person.

The upper half of the outer walls is covered with blue, green and white decorative tiles imported from Turkey in the 1960s. These tiles replaced the original ones which had deteriorated since the time they were affixed by Suleiman the Magnificent. The exterior was originally decorated with glass tiles. Verses from the Quran decorate the band around the top of the octagonal walls.

On the inside, every surface appears to be decorated with mosaics and geometrical designs. There is also a 787-foot- (240-m-) long inscription near the ceiling on both sides of the inner octagon, detailing information about the building and containing text from the Quran.

The plan of the Dome of the Rock consists of a circular dome-bearing drum, surrounded by two octagonal walls. Both the central high drum rests on piers and pillars as does the inner ambulatory. In 1994, King Hussein of Jordan funded the gilding of the dome with 24-karat gold.

The Rock (*as-Sakhra*)

The whole building is constructed round the Rock of biblical association. On entering (as tourists, only from the west), the starkness of its scarred surface contrasts strangely with the magnificence of the surroundings. It takes an exercise of the imagination to realize that this Rock is actually the top of Mount Moriah, where Abraham was sent to sacrifice his son Isaac. According to Jewish tradition, it was the same place where David later built an altar on the threshing floor of Araunah the Jebusite. As threshing floors are never built on

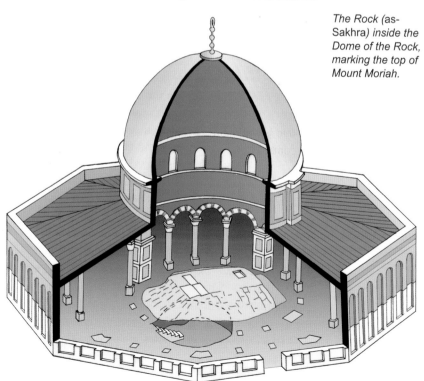

The Rock (as-Sakhra) inside the Dome of the Rock, marking the top of Mount Moriah.

An isometric drawing, viewed from the northwest, of the Rock with part of the floor of the Dome of the Rock omitted to show the full height of the western and northern scarps.

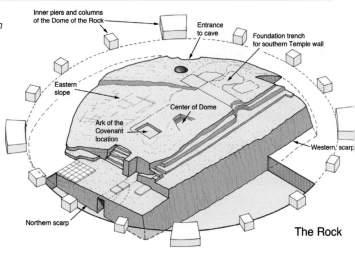

Inner piers and columns of the Dome of the Rock

Entrance to cave

Foundation trench for southern Temple wall

Eastern slope

Center of Dome

Ark of the Covenant location

Western scarp

Northern scarp

The Rock

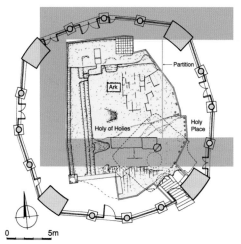

Partition

Ark

Holy of Holies

Holy Place

0   5m

The location of Solomon's Temple in relation to the Rock. The walls of Solomon's Temple are indicated in blue. After the destruction of the First Temple in 586 BCE, the Second Temple was built in the same location.

the peak of a mountain but rather a little to the east, the Rock must have been the place where Solomon built the Holy of Holies, so that the altar would have stood between the Dome of the Chain and the eastern arcade.

Facing opposite, behind the wooden fence, is the western face of the Rock with its flat top. On this side are two long steps carved by the Crusaders as foundations for a broad stairway that led up to the top of the Rock on which they built a large marble altar.

Walking round to the south, you reach an opening to an underground cave known as *al-Maghara*. This was a small natural cave, enlarged by the Crusaders and used to commemorate the angel's announcement to Zacharias that he would have a son (Luke 1.13). A hole is cut in the rocky ceiling to let the smoke from candles and incense escape.

Some have suggested that there might be another cave below the floor, the so-called *Bir al-Arwah* or the Well of Souls, but there is no evidence for this. On the contrary, an archaeologist who was present during renovation work a few decades ago noted that when the floor tiles had been pulled

The Rock as viewed from the ambulatory inside the Dome of the Rock.

up, only rock was seen a few inches below with no entrance to another cave.

Coming out of the cave, turn to the left (east). From this spot, one can see two flat rectangular areas cut in the rock. Leen Ritmeyer has identified these as foundation trenches for the south wall of the Holy of Holies of Solomon's Temple. They were cut to create a level surface on which to place the foundation stones of the Temple.

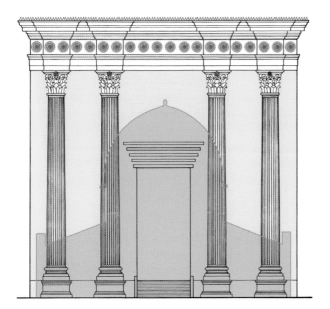

Drawing of the Temple façade and the silhouette of the Dome of the Rock (in blue). The height of Herod's Temple was 172 ft./52.5 m, one and a half times higher than the Dome of the Rock, which is 115 ft./35 m high.

On the eastern side, the Rock slopes down and quarry marks can be seen on its surface where the Crusaders had hewn off pieces to be sold as relics for their weight in gold. The upper level of the Rock can be better appreciated by examining the photograph (p.133) that was taken from high up under the dome. Two depressions are visible in the northern part. An artificially cut trapezoid indentation is located on a spot that can be calculated to be the very center of the Dome of the Rock. The most logical purpose of this was as the central pivot from which the plan of the Dome of the Rock was set out.

Just to the north of this is a rectangular depression that was the final one in a series of clues on the lunar-like rocky surface that allow us to decipher the history of the Rock. Using the flat areas on the south of the Rock together with the western and northern rockscarps, we can locate the original foundation walls of the Temple. The distance between the southern foundation trench and the northern rockscarp measured exactly 20 cubits (34 ft./

Artist's rendition of the Ark of the Covenant in the Holy of Holies, built on the Rock in the time of King Solomon.

For several years, renovation work was carried out on the mosaics of the inside of the cupola of the Dome of the Rock. As it was necessary to erect scaffolding on the Rock, it was temporarily deconsecrated. A colleague used this unique opportunity to walk on the Rock and take a close-up photograph of the "Mark of the Ark." (Photo: Marcio Teixeira)

10.5 m), the biblical dimensions given for the square Holy of Holies in 1 Kings 6.20. The measurements for the rectangular basin were 1.5 by 2.5 cubits, again the same measurements the Bible gives for the Ark of the Covenant (Exod 25.10). King Solomon records having "made a place" for the Ark in his Temple (1 Kgs 8.20–21). It is logical that such a sacred object could not be left to wobble about on the rocky surface that the Scripture reveals to have been left unfloored, but would need a stable base on which to stand. In addition to this, the indentation is located exactly in the center of the original projected Holy of Holies.

Drawing of the Veil in the Holy (Heikhal) of the Herodian Temple.

These clues, together with others, provided the basis for an analysis of the Rock and confirmed the placing of the Temple on the summit of Mount Moriah, as recorded by Josephus.

On the Day of Atonement, the High Priest would have walked up the eastern ramp to reach the Holy of Holies that, in Solomon's time, was separated from the Holy Place by a set of olive wooden doors (1 Kgs 6.31,32). The Deuteronomy Scroll written by Moses lay next to the Ark (Deut 31.26). After a period of neglect, this scroll was found by Hilkiah the High Priest when he cleansed the Temple on orders of King Josiah (2 Kgs 22.8).

In Herod's time, a 10-foot- (3-m-) high foundation platform was built around the Rock, so that it protruded only three fingerbreadths above the floor of the Holy of Holies (Mishnah, *Yoma* 5.2). The Ark of the Covenant was lost, thus the High Priest put incense in the emplacement of the Ark on the Day of Atonement. The Veil that separated the Holy from the Holy of Holies at that time, and which was torn from top to bottom when Jesus died (Luke 23:45), would have hung just below the eastern edge of the Rock.

16. SUMMER PULPIT (*MINBAR BURHAN AL-DIN*)

This ornate and beautiful structure, known as the Summer Pulpit, stands next to the southern arcade of the Raised Platform. A *minbar* is an essential piece of furniture in a mosque where the preacher stands to deliver his sermons. This one, built in the fourteenth century by the Muslim judge Burhan al-Din, is constructed out of stone and marble. It was used as an open-air platform to preach to the masses in the al-Aqsa Mosque on Fridays during the summer months. It contains many Crusader architectural elements and replaced a *minbar* originally made of wood and towed on wheels.

The Summer Pulpit.

The Southern Wall of the Raised Platform

Before descending the steps towards al-Aqsa, it is worthwhile to stop for a moment and reflect how the southern wall of the Raised Platform corresponds with the location of the steps that led up to the *hel*, the raised terrace of the Second Temple period. This terrace afforded access to several structures, such as the Kindling Gate, the Gate of the Firstlings and the Water Gate. The Jewish teachers used to instruct their students inside these areas, but on the high holidays they would go out and teach the common people. It was here that the 12-year-old Jesus listened to the teachers and asked them questions (Luke 2.46).

The level of the Raised Platform and the staircases that lead up to it are located at a slightly higher level than in the Herodian period. However, the present-day configuration of this platform still reflects a layout similar to that of the Second Temple period.

17. AL-KAS

The ornamental fountain at the foot of the stairway, called *al-Kas* (the Cup), was built in the Mamluk period. The taps around this basin are used for the washing of hands and feet before Muslim prayer. A new place for ablution is located nearby. *Al-Kas* receives its water from the Ottoman aqueduct that enters the Temple Mount over Wilson's Arch. The same aqueduct used to carry water to the large Cistern 8 (see plan of cisterns below, Appendix 2) on the Temple Mount during the Herodian period, when many small channels on the hill-

An atmospheric painting of the Great Sea (Cistern 8) by William Simpson, 1872.

The fountain of al-Kas (the Cup).

Al-Aqsa Mosque as viewed from the Mount of Olives, looking northwest.

slopes between Bethlehem and Hebron collected rainwater to the so-called Solomon's Pools south of Bethlehem. Several wellheads that belong to these cisterns can be seen to the east (see plan of Cisterns and Underground Structures, Appendix 2).

Al-Kas is located between two underground cisterns, nos. 6 and 36, that may have served as *mikva'ot* in the Second Temple period.

The olive tree just to the southeast of *al-Kas* is named after the Prophet Muhammad and has been linked to the Tree of Light mentioned in the Quran.

18. AL-AQSA MOSQUE

Looking southward, the large building in front of us with the lead-plated dome is the al-Aqsa Mosque. Whereas the Dome of the Rock was built as a shrine, this building is a place for prayer and study. The name al-Aqsa means "the farthest", and refers to Muhammad's Night Journey from Mecca to Jerusalem.

In 638 CE, a small timber mosque was built at the south end of the Temple Mount by Caliph Omar. Abd al-Malik, the builder of the Dome of the Rock, ordered it to be replaced by a stone building that was completed by his son al-Walid in 705 CE. This mosque was larger than the one we see today. It had seven aisles on both sides of the central nave and could accommodate up to 5,000 worshippers.

The mosque was destroyed by earthquakes in 746, 1033 and 1927. The plan of the present mosque has only three aisles on either side of the nave.

During the Crusader period, the mosque served as a palace and headquarters of the Knights Templar. Its name was then changed to *Templum Salomonis* (the Temple of Solomon).

In July 1951, King Abdullah, the first king of Transjordan, was assassinated at the entrance to the al-Aqsa Mosque during Friday prayers. His grandson, Hussein, who was to

Main entrance to al-Aqsa Mosque.

Stairway that descends to the underground passageway of the Double Gate.

Queen Melisende of Jerusalem

Queen Melisende (married to Fulk of Anjou) inherited the crown of the Crusader Kingdom from her father King Baldwin II and ruled from 1131 to 1153. She was one of the greatest art patrons of the Latin Kingdom during the twelfth century and sponsored the great ironwork grille that encircled the Rock up to about 1960.

become King of Jordan, was beside him at the time. The story goes that a bullet was deflected by a medal pinned to Hussein's chest on the insistence of his grandfather, thus saving the future king's life.

To the east of the main entrance is a stairway that descends to an area underneath the al-Aqsa. This is the site of the underground passageway from the Second Temple period that led to the Double Gate. Its southern end has remained intact, complete with four beautifully sculptured domes. This was the main southern entrance to the Temple court.

19. ISLAMIC MUSEUM

To the west of the al-Aqsa are some buildings of Crusader origin which have been transformed into a complex known as the al-Aqsa Library and the Islamic Museum. Entry is forbidden to non-Muslims. The complex contains a valuable collection of Qurans and Islamic documents dealing with various aspects of life in Jerusalem. An interesting piece of metalwork displayed in the museum is a grille which was placed around the Rock inside the Dome of the Rock in the Crusader period and was only removed to the museum in the nineteenth century. Another relic is a pair of metal candlesticks in the shape of a pomegranate tree, also dating to the Crusader period and originating in the Dome of the Rock. The courtyard outside the museum displays architectural elements from the various periods. They include a Herodian sarcophagus, the wellhead of Cistern 20 (see plan of cisterns below, Appendix 2), and Byzantine and Crusader column capitals.

Here ends your visit, but this quiet spot provides a convenient place to stop and reflect on a tour that has brought you around, under and on top of this Mountain of the House of the Lord. Even if political conditions prevent you from visiting all or part of it, our circuit of the Temple Mount will have given you a deeper insight into its recesses and secret places and make it easier for you to "Let Jerusalem come into your mind" (Jeremiah 51.50).

The courtyard of the Islamic Museum on the Temple Mount, with architectural remains on display.

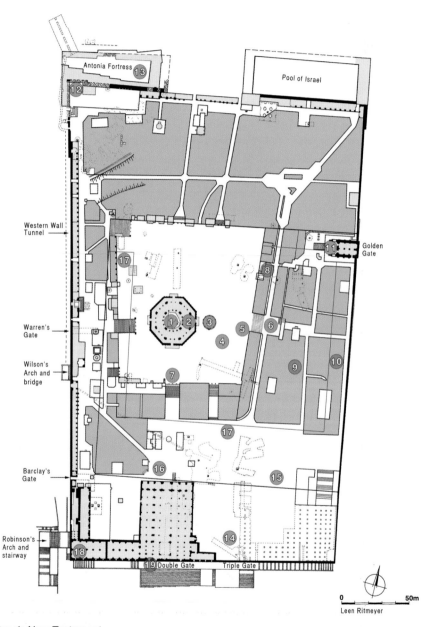

Antonia Fortress ⑬

Pool of Israel

⑫

Western Wall Tunnel

Golden Gate

⑪

⑰

⑧

Warren's Gate

① ② ③

④

⑤

⑥

Wilson's Arch and bridge

⑨

⑩

⑦

⑰

Barclay's Gate

⑯

⑮

⑭

Robinson's Arch and stairway

⑱

⑲ Double Gate   Triple Gate

0   50m

Leen Ritmeyer

Plan 1: New Testament
links to the present-day
Temple Mount.

TWO PLANS OF NEW TESTAMENT LINKS TO THE TEMPLE MOUNT

KEY TO PLANS AND DESCRIPTION

Jesus said: "Did you not know that I must be in my Father's house?" (Luke 2.49 ESV)

(The list below includes references to the Mishnah and the Talmud, in italics, and to the Old Testament, where additional information to that provided in the New Testament is needed.)

1. Location of the Holy of Holies
- There was no Ark of the Covenant here in the first century

2. Holy Place
- Zacharias sees the angel Gabriel on the right side of the Altar of Incense (Luke 1.9–20; *Tamid* 5.6)
- The Veil between the Holy Place and the Holy of Holies was torn when Jesus died (Matthew 27.51; Mark 15.38; Luke 23:45; *Shekalim* 8.5)

3. Location of the Porch with the Golden Vine
- Jesus said: I am the Vine… (John 15.1; *Middot* 3.8)
- The Priestly Blessing was recited here (Luke 1.22; Numbers 6.24–26; *Tamid* 7.2)

4. Location of the Altar
- Offering a gift at the Altar (Matthew 5.23,24)
- Swearing by the Altar (Matthew 23.18–20)
- Zacharias was murdered between the Temple and the Altar (Matthew 23.35; Luke 11.51)
- Priests serve at the Altar (1 Corinthians 9.13)
- Jesus refers to the water-drawing ceremony of the Feast of Tabernacles (John 7.37–38)
- Sacrificing of the Passover lamb (Matthew 26.19; Mark 14.12; Luke 22.7; 1 Corinthians 5.7; *Pesahim* 5.5–8)

5. The southern side gate of the Nicanor Gate
- Mary watched her sacrifice of 2 pigeons being sacrificed on the Altar from this location (Luke 2.22–24; *Kinnim* 3.6)

6. Location of Court of the Women (most gatherings on the Temple took place here, the Treasury being located under the colonnade that surrounded the Court of the Women)
- Presentation of Jesus and meeting with Simeon and Anna the Prophetess (Luke 2.25–38)

- Jesus teaches in the Temple (Matthew 21.23; John 7.14,28; John 8.2,20)
- Jesus declares himself "the light of the world" (John 8.12)
- The rich putting their gifts into the Treasury contrasted with the widow's two mites (Luke 21.1–4)
- Children shouting in the Temple: "Hosanna to the Son of David" during the Triumphal Entry (Matthew 21.15)
- Judas casts the price of blood into the Temple Treasury (Matthew 27.5)
- Peter and John preach here as commanded by the angel of the Lord (Acts 5.20,42)

7. Terrace (Hebrew: *hel*)

- Young Jesus sat here among the teachers at Passover (Luke 2.46; Babylonian Talmud, *Sanhedrin* 88b)

8. Chamber of the Lepers

- Place for healed lepers to be examined (Matthew 8.2–4; *Middot* 2.5)

9. Chamber of the Nazarites

- Paul, with four other men, almost completes his Nazarite vow, but is seized in the Temple before he can do so (Acts 21.26,27; *Middot* 2.5; *Nazir* 1.1)

10. Solomon's Porch

- Jesus walked in Solomon's Colonnade during the Feast of Dedication (Hanukkah) (John 10.23)
- People gather here after the healing of the lame man (Acts 3.11)
- Peter and John seized here and put in jail (Acts 4.1–3)
- Regular meeting place for believers (Acts 2.46; 5.12)

11. Shushan Gate

- The scapegoat was led out through this gate (Leviticus 16.21,22; Hebrews 9.28; *Yoma* 6.3,4)

12. Stairs leading up to the Antonia Fortress

- Paul stands above the stairs and speaks to the Jewish people (Acts 21.40)

13. Antonia Fortress

- Paul kept in the Antonia (Acts 22.24; 23.10)
- The son of Paul's sister heard of the plot to kill Paul and went into the barracks (Antonia) to warn him (Acts 23.16)
- Paul taken from the Antonia to Antipatris (Acts 23.31)

14. Royal Stoa

- Usual location of money-changers and sellers of doves

15. Location of the sacred Mishnaic 500-cubit-square Temple Mount

- Only this square area was considered holy by the religious authorities of the first century

16. Inside the sacred area

- Jesus drives out all who bought and sold in the Temple, overthrows the tables of the money-changers and overturns the seats of those selling doves (Matthew 21.12; Mark 11.15; Luke 19.45; John 2.14–15)

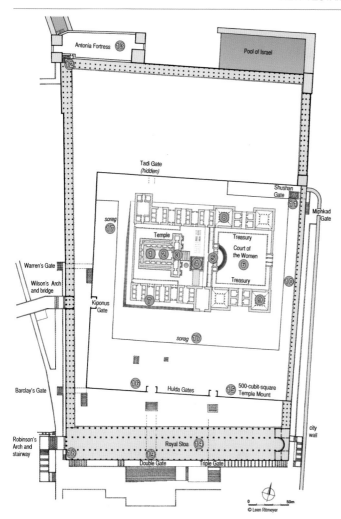

Plan 2: New Testament links to the Herodian Temple Mount.

17. *Soreg*, or dividing wall of hostility (middle wall of partition, KJV)
- Broken down by Jesus (Ephesians 2.14; *Middot* 2.3)

18. Pinnacle
- Place for the blowing of trumpets (Numbers 10.2,10)
- Jesus is tempted to throw himself down (Matthew 4.5; Luke 4.9)

19. Beautiful Gate (Double Gate)
- Jesus heals the blind and the lame (Matthew 21.14)
- Peter and John heal the lame man at the Beautiful Gate (Acts 3.1–11)

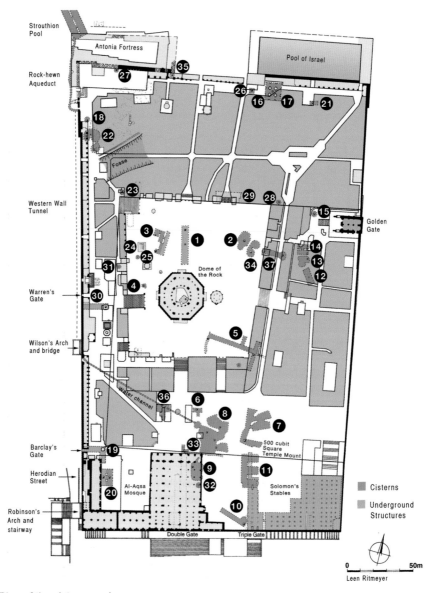

*Plan of the cisterns and
underground structures
according to the
numeration of Warren.*

PLAN OF THE CISTERNS AND UNDERGROUND STRUCTURES

KEY TO PLAN AND DESCRIPTION

1. Tadi Gate underground passageway and *hypogeion* of the Hasmonean *Baris*, later used as a cistern.

2. Cistern in the northern court of the square Temple Mount, located below the Gate of the Flame.

3. Bathing complex used by the priests, including at least one *mikveh*, probably located in the westernmost chamber. The eastern chamber was an underground passageway connected with the Tadi Gate.

4. Retort-shaped cistern, located in the western part of the square Temple Mount, between the *soreg* and the Temple Court.

5. Large passageway-shaped cistern, known as "The Well of the Pomegranate." Its western wellhead was located inside the Water Gate near the Altar. The water of this cistern was probably used in ceremonies connected with the Altar and the Laver and may be identified with the "*Golah Cistern*" of Mishnah, *Erubin* 10.14.

6. T-shaped cistern east of *al-Kas* (The Cup). May have been used as a *mikveh* in the southern court of the square Temple Mount.

7. Very large cistern known as "The Sea". It was probably the reservoir excavated by Simon the High Priest in 200 BCE, as mentioned by Ben Sira in *Ecclesiasticus* 50.3. Located in the southern court of the square Temple Mount. The stones that were quarried when the cistern was made were probably used to repair the Temple in Simon's time.

8. Largest cistern called "The Great Sea" with a capacity of 2 million gallons of water. It may be identified with the "Great Cistern" mentioned in Mishnah, *Erubin* 10.14. It is located in the southern court of the square Temple Mount, west of Cistern 7.

9. Cistern called "The Well of the Leaf." Located in the Hasmonean extension of the square Temple Mount.

10. Passageway-shaped cistern near the Triple Gate. Connected with rock-cut channels that run under the Herodian Southern Wall below the Triple Gate. Located below the Herodian Royal Stoa.

11. Large E-shaped cistern. May be identified with "The Cistern of the *Akra*," mentioned in *Erubin* 10.14.

12, 13, 14. Cisterns located in the northern court of the square Temple Mount, below the

Court of the Women and the Chamber of the Woodshed.

15. Cistern located just inside the northern boundary wall of the square Temple Mount.

16, 17. Vaulted cistern with two wellheads, of medieval construction.

18. Cistern, which in pre-Herodian times received water from the Rock-hewn Aqueduct that conveyed water from the northern Tyropoeon Valley. Located in the northern extension of Herod's Temple Mount.

19. Barclay's Gate underground passageway.

20. Southern continuation of Barclay's Gate passageway.

21. Small cistern, probably of medieval construction.

22. Large pre-Herodian cistern with domed roof and rock-cut staircase running around its wall, which probably also received water from the Rock-hewn Aqueduct (see Cistern 18).

23. Cistern located at the northwest corner of the square Temple Mount, presumably inside a tower.

24. Relatively modern chamber, the eastern wall of which is a rockscarp that may be linked with the location of the *soreg*.

25. Cistern in the western court of the square Temple Mount, outside the *soreg*.

26. Small cistern, probably of medieval date.

27. Small cistern at the southern base of the Antonia Fortress.

28. Small cistern just outside the northern boundary wall of the square Temple Mount, known as "The Well of the Abyssinian." It may have been located inside a tower.

29. Masonry chamber, built against the northern rockscarp of the square Temple Mount, probably part of the Crusader "Monastery of the Temple." The bedrock projections from the northern boundary wall of the Raised Platform may indicate an identification with the Prison Gate mentioned in Nehemiah 12.39.

30. Warren's Gate underground passageway. Probably part of an L-shaped construction similar to Barclay's Gate passageway. Here, however, the second leg had been later filled in.

31. Cistern which falls just inside the Western Wall of the square Temple Mount.

32. Small cistern beneath the al-Aqsa Mosque.

33. Small cistern north of the al-Aqsa Mosque, located under the steps leading down to the Double Gate underground passageway. This cistern is located inside the Hasmonean extension to the square Temple Mount.

34. Cistern in the northern part of the Temple Court, located below the Gate of the Flame.

35. Small cistern located near the eastern side of the Antonia Fortress.

36. T-shaped cistern west of *al-Kas*. Like Cistern 6, this cistern may have been used as a *mikveh* in the southern court of the square Temple Mount.

37. Cistern in the northern court of the square Temple Mount (explored by C. Schick), located in the Court of the Women.

PLAN OF MUSLIM BUILDINGS

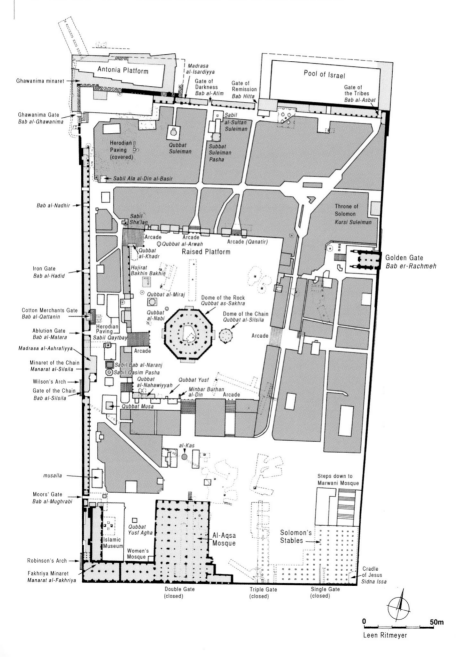

Ghawanima minaret

Ghawanima Gate
Bab al-Ghawanima

Antonia Platform

Madrasa al-Isardiyya

Gate of Darkness
Bab al-Atim

Gate of Remission
Bab Hitta

Pool of Israel

Gate of the Tribes
Bab al-Asbat

Sabil al-Sultan Suleiman

Herodian Paving (covered)

Qubbat Suleiman

Subbat Suleiman Pasha

Sabil Ala al-Din al-Basir

Bab al-Nadhir

Sabil Sha'lan

Throne of Solomon
Kursi Suleiman

Arcade Arcade
Qubbat al-Arwah
Qubbat al-Khadr

Arcade (Qanatir)

Raised Platform

Golden Gate
Bab er-Rachmeh

Iron Gate
Bab al-Hadid

Hujirat Bakhin Bakhin

Qubbat al-Miraj

Cotton Merchants Gate
Bab al-Qattanin

Qubbat al-Nabi

Herodian Paving
Sabil Qaytbay

Ablution Gate
Bab al-Matara

Arcade

Madrasa al-Ashrafiyya

Minaret of the Chain
Manarat al-Silsila

Wilson's Arch

Gate of the Chain
Bab al-Silsila

Dome of the Rock
Qubbat as-Sakhra

Dome of the Chain
Qubbat al-Silsila

Arcade

Sabil Bab al-Naranj
Sabil Qasim Pasha

Qubbat al-Nahawiyyah

Qubbat Yusf

Minbar Burhan al-Din

Arcade

Qubbat Musa

al-Kas

Steps down to Marwani Mosque

musalla

Moors' Gate
Bab al-Mughrabi

Qubbat Yusf Agha

Solomon's Stables

Islamic Museum

Al-Aqsa Mosque

Robinson's Arch

Women's Mosque

Fakhriya Minaret
Manarat al-Fakhriya

Cradle of Jesus
Sidna Issa

Double Gate (closed)

Triple Gate (closed)

Single Gate (closed)

0   50m

Leen Ritmeyer

GLOSSARY OF ARCHAEOLOGICAL AND ARCHITECTURAL TERMS

[1]Acanthus: a plant with large scalloped leaves, the stylized form of which is used as a motif in Corinthian and composite capitals

Aisle: the part of a basilica that is separated from the central nave by a row of columns

Ambulatory: a walkway round the inside of a dome or cloister

Apse: a vaulted semi-circular recess located at the end of a basilica or church

Arabesque: intricate surface decoration based on geometrical patterns of scrolls, foliage or tendrils

Ashlars: hewn blocks of stone, precisely squared and usually with drafted margins, laid in horizontal courses with fine vertical joints

Basilica: a large meeting hall, divided into a central nave and two or more aisles separated by rows of columns

Boss: the central part of an ashlar that projects above the margins

Buttress: masonry built against a wall to give additional strength

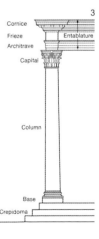

Capital: the crowning feature of a column or pilaster. In classical architecture there are three dominant orders: Doric, [2]Ionic and [3]Corinthian. Each system uses capitals and other architectural elements needed to assemble a column in a different style.

Colonnade: a series of columns carrying an entablature or arches

Corbel: a projecting stone or console supporting a beam or other horizontal structure

Cornice: a projecting ornamental molding along the top of a building

Crepidoma: a stepped platform on which a Greek or Roman temple is constructed

Cruciform: in the shape of a cross

Cubit: an ancient unit of length, measuring 18 inches/45cm from elbow to fingertip. The sacred or royal cubit was four fingers longer (20.67 inches/52.5cm) and was used in the design of religious or public buildings

Cupola: a small dome on top of a roof or other structure

Entablature: the upper part of an architectural order, consisting of an architrave, frieze and cornice

Facsimile: a copy or reproduction of an ancient artifact

Fosse: an excavated ditch or moat used for defence

Frieze: the frequently decorated middle part of an entablature, located between the architrave and cornice

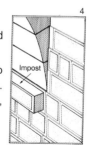

[4]**Impost:** a projecting block of stone on which the end of an arch rests. To construct a stone arch, a wooden arch was first placed on the imposts. After the stone arch was built, the wooden support was taken down, leaving the imposts in place

Lintel: a horizontal stone or beam bridging an opening

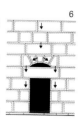

[5]*Mikveh* (plural: *mikva'ot*): in Judaism, a bath for ritual immersion

Mosaic: a decoration for walls or floors made of small pieces (*tesserae*) of stone or glass set in mortar

Nave: the central part of a basilica type building, flanked by aisles

Offset: a part of a wall that projects from the adjacent masonry

Palmette: a fan-shaped decoration composed of narrow divisions like a palm leaf

Parapet: a low wall for protection at the edge of a balcony or rooftop

Pier: a solid, freestanding masonry support, usually rectangular in shape

Pilaster: a shallow rectangular or semi-circular column projecting slightly from a wall

Pivot: a fixed point around which something rotates, or a pin or shaft from which a circle can be set out

Porch: a covered entrance to a building

Portico: a roofed space either open or partly enclosed and usually supported by columns

[6]**Relieving arch:** an arch placed over a lintel to relieve the pressure from the weight of the wall above

Reliquary: a container for relics, usually placed under an altar in a church

Retaining wall: a wall that supports a weight of earth or fill. It may be battered, with the face inclined toward the load it is bearing.

Rosette: a rose shaped circular ornament, decorated with leaves or petals

Sarcophagus: (Greek for "flesh-eating") a stone coffin, frequently decorated and carrying inscriptions

Scallop: a decoration imitating the shape of a shell

Scarp: a steep slope or rock face

Stoa: a detached colonnade or hall with a roof supported by one or more rows of columns parallel to the rear wall

Select Bibliography

Bahat, D., *The Carta Jerusalem Atlas*, Jerusalem (2011).

Bahat, D., *The Jerusalem Western Wall Tunnel*, Jerusalem (2013).

Ben-Dov, M., *In the Shadow of the Temple*, Jerusalem (1982).

Burgoyne, Michael H., *Mamluk Jerusalem*, Buckhurst Hill (1987).

Creswell, Keppel A. C., *Early Muslim Architecture*, Oxford (1969).

Gibson, S., and D. M. Jacobson, *Below the Temple Mount in Jerusalem*, Oxford (1996).

Gonen, R, *Contested Holiness: Jewish, Muslim, and Christian Perspective on the Temple Mount in Jerusalem*, Jersey City (2003).

Grabar, O., *The Shape of the Holy—Early Islamic Jerusalem*, Princeton (1996).

Grabar, O., *The Dome of the Rock*, Princeton (2006).

Mazar, B., *The Mountain of the Lord*, New York (1975).

Mazar, E., *The Complete Guide to the Temple Mount Excavations*, Jerusalem (2002).

Mazar, E., *The Walls of the Temple Mount*, Jerusalem (2011)

Netzer, E., "The Rebuilding of the Second Temple and its Precinct" in *The Architecture of Herod the Great Builder*, Grand Rapids (2006).

Price, R., *Rose Guide to the Temple*, Torrance (2012).

Ritmeyer, L. & K., *The Ritual of the Temple in the Time of Christ*, Jerusalem (2002).

Ritmeyer, L. & K., *Secrets of Jerusalem's Temple Mount*, Updated and Enlarged Edition, Washington, D.C. (2006).

Ritmeyer, L., *The Quest—Revealing the Temple Mount in Jerusalem*, Jerusalem (2006).

Ritmeyer, L. & K., *Jerusalem in the Time of Nehemiah*, Jerusalem (2014).

Ritmeyer, L. & K., *Jerusalem in the Year 30 A.D.*, Jerusalem (2014).

Reich, R., G. Avni, and T. Winter, *The Jerusalem Archaeological Park*, Jerusalem (1999).

SOURCE INDEX

OLD TESTAMENT

NEW TESTAMENT

MISHNAH AND TALMUD

JOSEPHUS

GENERAL INDEX

The Arabic definite articles (*al-*, *as-*, etc.) are disregarded in the alphabetical listing.